Learn Spanish Faster: The Hyperspeed Method for Beginners Who Want Real Results

Prof. Alejandro Morales

Table of contents

Introduction

Language is not a subject. It's a skill. That sentence matters more than it looks like it should, because it quietly dismantles almost everything you've been taught about how learning a language is supposed to work. Subjects are studied, memorized, examined, and then mostly forgotten. Skills are trained. They are messy at the beginning, uncomfortable in the middle, and deeply satisfying once they start to move on their own. No one "studies" balance before riding a bike, or conjugates muscle fibers before learning to swim. You practice, you wobble, you fall, you adjust. You get feedback quickly, sometimes painfully, and your body and mind adapt. Language works the same way, yet we persist in treating it like a history exam: long study sessions, delayed feedback, and the quiet hope that fluency will emerge someday as a reward for patience. It usually doesn't. Skills grow fastest when the loop between action and correction is short. Speak, notice what breaks, adjust, speak again. This is the advantage you're about to use.

Spanish Flow is not about sounding impressive or erasing your accent or reaching some imaginary finish line called "native-level." It's about speed, clarity, and confidence arriving together, not one day at a time over years, but week by week through deliberate exposure. Speed does not mean rushing your words; it means your brain stops freezing when it needs to respond. Clarity does not mean perfect grammar; it means the other person understands you without effort or confusion. Confidence does not mean fear disappears; it means fear stops controlling your choices. When these three move in sync, something changes. Conversations stop feeling like tests. Spanish stops feeling like a foreign object you're holding at arm's length and starts behaving like a tool you can actually use. Perfection is not only unnecessary, it is actively unhelpful at the beginning. Waiting to be correct before being fluent is like waiting to be strong before lifting weights.

The next sixty days are designed around a simple idea: frequency beats duration, and feedback beats theory. Instead of heroic study sessions that exhaust your motivation and then disappear from your schedule, you'll work with daily micro-habits that fit into real life. Small actions, done consistently, reshape your instincts. You will speak from the very first day, not because you're ready, but because readiness is a consequence of action, not a prerequisite. Weekly checkpoints will prevent you from drifting into the comforting illusion of "I'm learning, but I'm not ready to talk yet." Each checkpoint exists to answer one question only: can you do more now than you could seven days ago, under light pressure, without preparation? If the answer is yes, you're winning. If it's no, the system adjusts. There is no shame in adjustment; rigidity is the real enemy of progress.

Talking from Day 1 is not a motivational slogan. It is a neurological shortcut. Your brain prioritizes what feels immediately relevant and socially meaningful. Silent study tells your brain that Spanish is abstract, theoretical, and optional. Speaking, even clumsily, tells your brain that Spanish is alive, relational, and urgent. When you struggle to find a word mid-sentence, you create a gap your brain is highly motivated to close. When you mispronounce something and are still understood, you weaken the belief that mistakes are dangerous. When you freeze and then recover, you build resilience rather than avoidance. None of this happens in isolation with a textbook. Flow is not memorized; it's conditioned.

Before you start building anything, though, you need to know what you're building on. Everyone arrives at Spanish with a personal baseline, and ignoring it is one of the fastest ways to sabotage progress. Your baseline is not your vocabulary size or your grammar knowledge. It's your internal response to pressure. Some people tense up when they can't find a word and their mind goes blank. Others rush, overtalk, and lose coherence. Some apologize constantly, shrinking their presence with every sentence. Others default to silence, hoping the conversation will move on without them. These reactions are not flaws in intelligence or talent. They are stress responses. If you don't identify yours, they will quietly run the show.

Confidence blockers often disguise themselves as standards. You might tell yourself you need to "know more" before speaking, or that your accent is embarrassing, or that you don't want to bother people. Underneath those stories is usually a simpler fear: losing face, sounding foolish, being judged. The problem is not that these fears exist; it's that they remain unnamed. When unnamed, they feel like truth. When named, they become variables you can work with. Over the next sixty days, you will not try to eliminate fear. You will train while it's present. Confidence will emerge as a side effect of repeated survival, not as a feeling you wait for before acting.

Equally important is defining your minimum viable Spanish. This is the smallest version of Spanish that still works for your real life. It is not everything you might someday want to say; it is what you need to say now to function, connect, and not feel helpless. Maybe it's ordering food without switching to English. Maybe it's holding a five-minute conversation about your work. Maybe it's expressing disagreement politely instead of nodding along. Most learners never define this, so they drown in possibilities and measure themselves against an undefined ideal. By naming your minimum viable Spanish, you give your practice direction. You stop chasing "more" and start consolidating "enough." Ironically, this is what accelerates growth.

The sixty-day structure is intentionally finite. Open-ended goals invite procrastination. A clear time boundary sharpens focus. You are not committing to becoming fluent forever; you are committing to showing up today, and then tomorrow, inside a container that is designed to be survivable. Daily habits will be small enough that you can't argue your way out of them. Weekly reflections will be honest enough that you can't lie to yourself about what's working. Speaking will be frequent enough that your nervous system adapts instead of panics. This is not a challenge in discipline; it is an experiment in design. When the environment supports the behavior, motivation becomes far less important.

You may notice early resistance. It might sound like boredom, or skepticism, or the urge to "optimize" before you begin. This is normal. Skills threaten identities. If you have been the person who "knows Spanish but doesn't speak it," this process will gently dismantle that label. If you have been the person who avoids situations where Spanish is required, you will start stepping into them in controlled doses. Expect friction. Friction is evidence that something real is happening. Comfort rarely produces change.

By the end of these sixty days, the goal is not mastery. The goal is momentum. Spanish should feel less like an obstacle and more like a moving walkway you've learned how to step onto. You should recognize your stress patterns as they arise instead of being hijacked by them. You should trust that you can enter a conversation, get lost, and find your way back out again. Flow is not the absence of pauses; it's the absence of panic when pauses occur.

This introduction is not here to inspire you. Inspiration fades. It's here to reframe what you're about to do so you don't sabotage it with the wrong expectations. Language grows through use, not preparation. Feedback works best when it's immediate, not delayed. Confidence is built through exposure, not affirmation. Over the next sixty days, you will not wait until Spanish feels easy. You will make it familiar. And familiarity, practiced daily under light pressure, is what quietly turns effort into flow.

Chapter 1 — The Confidence Engine: Speak Before You're Ready

1.1 The "Permission to Be Bad" Rule

Most people don't fail at learning Spanish because they lack intelligence, time, or even motivation. They fail because they never grant themselves permission to sound bad long enough to become good. Somewhere early on, usually after a few classes or a few awkward attempts, an invisible rule takes over: don't speak until you can do it properly. The problem is that this rule feels reasonable. It sounds mature. It sounds respectful. In reality, it quietly shuts down the very mechanism that builds confidence. Speaking is not the reward at the end of learning; it is the engine that powers the entire process.

Research on skill acquisition has repeated this lesson across fields as different as music, sports, and public speaking. Early, imperfect practice creates faster and more durable progress than delayed, polished performance. The reason is simple and uncomfortable: skills are not built by knowing what to do, but by experiencing what happens when you try. For speaking skills in particular, waiting until you "know enough" creates a double penalty. You don't train the motor patterns of speech, and you reinforce the belief that mistakes are dangerous. Over time, that belief becomes heavier than the language itself.

The "Permission to Be Bad" rule exists to break that loop. It is not a mindset trick or a motivational phrase. It is an operational rule that changes how you behave under pressure. You decide in advance that sounding incomplete, slow, or incorrect is not a failure condition. Silence is. This one shift reorders your priorities. Your goal stops being to impress and starts being to participate. Participation, repeated often enough, does something subtle to your nervous system. Spanish stops triggering a threat response and starts registering as a familiar, survivable environment.

To understand why this matters, imagine trying to learn to swim by reading about strokes while standing on the edge of the pool. You could memorize every movement, every breathing pattern, every safety rule, and still freeze the moment you touch the water. Speaking a language works the same way. Until you experience the sensation of not knowing a word and continuing anyway, you don't actually know how to speak. You only know how to prepare. The permission to be bad is the step that gets you into the water.

This permission becomes actionable through scripts. Not scripts in the theatrical sense, but simple, reusable openings that let you start speaking with far less than you think you need. Most beginners wait for a large vocabulary before attempting real speech, but conversation does not require abundance. It requires continuity. With fifty words and a handful of connectors, you can already communicate presence, intention, and basic meaning. The secret is not variety, but recombination. The same few verbs, pronouns, and fillers can carry you through hundreds of exchanges if you stop trying to say everything and start saying something.

A starting script does not aim for elegance. It aims for momentum. "I am learning Spanish." "I don't know the word." "Can you repeat?" "I think that…" These phrases are not signs of weakness; they are structural supports. They keep you speaking when your vocabulary runs out. They also send a clear signal to the other person that communication is a shared responsibility, not a performance you must carry alone. Once you internalize a few of these openings, the fear of starting a conversation drops dramatically, because starting no longer feels like a cliff. It feels like stepping onto a familiar path.

The moment you open your mouth, another trap appears: translation. Many learners believe fluency is about finding the perfect Spanish equivalent for their thoughts in another language. This belief slows everything down. It creates pauses that feel like failure and reinforces the idea that speaking is mentally expensive. The "Permission to Be Bad" rule pairs naturally with the three-second rule to counter this. When a question is asked, or when it's your turn to speak, you respond within three seconds, even if the response is simple, incomplete, or slightly off. You are not allowed to wait for the perfect sentence. You say the first workable version that appears.

This does two important things. First, it trains speed. Fluency is not the absence of errors; it is the absence of paralysis. By responding quickly, you teach your brain that Spanish is something you act in, not something you solve. Second, it weakens the translation habit. When you don't give yourself time to build sentences in your head, you start reaching for direct associations instead. Words connect to meanings, not to other words. This is how children learn, and it is how adults relearn when they stop overcontrolling the process.

At first, the three-second rule will feel reckless. You may worry about saying the wrong thing, sounding abrupt, or missing nuance. These concerns are understandable, but they are misplaced at this stage. Nuance comes from exposure, not hesitation. Politeness comes from tone, not grammatical perfection. Most importantly, conversations are forgiving environments. People are far more focused on understanding you than on evaluating you. When you respond quickly and keep going, you project engagement. Engagement covers many sins.

Over time, something interesting happens. Your responses begin to speed up without effort. You stop feeling the internal countdown because your brain no longer needs it. This is not because you suddenly know more words, but because the pathway from thought to speech has been exercised. Just as a musician's fingers learn where to go without conscious planning, your mouth learns how to move without negotiation. This is what confidence feels like from the inside: not certainty, but continuity.

Measuring progress in this phase requires a different kind of honesty. Traditional metrics focus on vocabulary size, grammar accuracy, or test scores. These are lagging indicators. They change slowly and often fail to capture what actually matters in conversation. Confidence grows through courage, not accumulation. That is why you need confidence trackers that measure behavior under pressure rather than knowledge on paper.

A confidence tracker asks questions like these: Did you speak when it would have been easier to stay silent? Did you respond even when you weren't sure? Did you recover after getting stuck instead of switching languages or withdrawing? These moments are small, but they are the building blocks of real fluency. Each time you choose participation over protection, you reinforce a new identity. You are no longer someone who is "learning Spanish someday." You are someone who uses Spanish now, imperfectly, but willingly.

Tracking courage also reframes failure. If you judge yourself by correctness, every mistake feels like a step backward. If you judge yourself by engagement, mistakes become evidence of effort. This shift matters because language learning is emotionally noisy. There will be days when words vanish, when fatigue slows you down, when you feel less capable than the week before. Without the right metric, these days can undo your motivation. With it, they become neutral data points. You spoke. You stayed in the conversation. The engine kept running.

The deeper effect of the "Permission to Be Bad" rule is psychological. It separates your self-worth from your performance. Many adults carry an unspoken belief that sounding incompetent threatens their identity. In familiar contexts, this belief stays hidden. In a new language, it comes roaring to the surface. By choosing to speak before you're ready, you confront that belief directly. You discover that embarrassment is survivable, that misunderstandings can be repaired, that respect is not earned through perfection but through presence.

This discovery doesn't happen all at once. It accumulates quietly. One conversation where you stumble and recover. One interaction where you are understood despite errors. One moment where you realize the fear has softened, not because it disappeared, but because you stopped obeying it. Over time, these moments change how you see yourself. Confidence stops being something you wait for and becomes something you practice.

The confidence engine runs on action, not affirmation. You don't become confident and then speak. You speak, and confidence catches up. The "Permission to Be Bad" rule ensures that the engine actually turns over instead of stalling at the starting line. When you accept that early speech will be messy, you remove the final excuse for delay. You step into the conversation as you are, not as you wish to be. And that, paradoxically, is what allows growth to begin.

By the end of this chapter, the goal is not that you feel fearless. The goal is that you feel authorized. Authorized to speak with limited tools. Authorized to respond quickly. Authorized to measure progress by courage rather than correctness. Once that authorization is internal, Spanish stops being a test you're preparing for and becomes a space you're already inhabiting. The engine is on. Now it can build speed.

1.2 Anxiety-Proofing Your Brain

If confidence is the engine, anxiety is the friction that keeps it from running smoothly. Most people experience it not as fear in the abstract, but as a very specific physical and mental shutdown. You know the moment: a simple question is asked, one you could probably answer on paper, and suddenly your mind goes empty. Your chest tightens, your breathing shortens, and the words you were sure you knew scatter. This is not a failure of memory or intelligence. It is a freeze response, and it is entirely predictable.

The freeze response is the brain's attempt to protect you from perceived threat. In everyday life, it activates during social evaluation, uncertainty, and time pressure. Speaking a foreign language combines all three. Your brain does not distinguish between "I might sound foolish" and "I might be in danger" as clearly as you would like. When it senses risk, it prioritizes safety over creativity. Blood flow shifts away from the areas responsible for flexible language and toward systems designed for survival. The result is silence, rigidity, or a sudden urge to escape the situation.

Anxiety-proofing your brain does not mean eliminating this response. That would be unrealistic. It means learning how to move through it instead of being trapped by it. The most effective way to do that is not through reassurance, but through patterning. When your brain freezes, it needs something automatic to grab onto, something that does not require invention. This is where simple speech patterns come in. Short, reusable structures give your mind a rail to hold while the rest of the system catches up.

These patterns are deliberately unsophisticated. They are not there to impress, but to re-establish motion. Phrases that buy time, signal effort, or name difficulty out loud do more than fill space. They reframe the moment from a private failure into a shared process. When you say that you are thinking, that you are searching for a word, or that you are not sure but will try, you interrupt the freeze. You are no longer trapped inside your head, silently evaluating yourself. You are back in interaction.

What matters is not the exact wording, but the function. The function is to keep sound coming out of your mouth while your brain regains flexibility. Silence, especially unintentional silence, reinforces panic. Sound interrupts it. Even imperfect sound. Even repetitive sound. Over time, your nervous system learns a new association: forgetting a word does not equal danger; it equals a small detour that can be navigated.

This is also why building a safe practice environment is not optional. Anxiety decreases fastest when exposure happens in conditions that are predictable and forgiving. Many learners assume the opposite, throwing themselves into high-stakes situations too early and then concluding they are "bad at languages" when it goes poorly. A safe environment does not mean an easy one. It means one where the cost of error is low and the opportunity for repetition is high.

Solo speaking is one of the most underestimated tools in this process. Speaking out loud to yourself may feel artificial at first, but neurologically it is powerful. Your brain does not fully differentiate between imagined social interaction and real one when language is involved. When you speak alone, you train the motor patterns of speech without the added load of social judgment. You learn what it feels like to hear yourself produce Spanish continuously. This familiarity reduces shock when you speak with others.

Solo speaking also allows you to rehearse recovery. You can deliberately practice getting stuck and then restarting. You can pause mid-sentence, lose a word on purpose, and then use a recovery phrase to continue. This trains resilience, not avoidance. By the time it happens in a real conversation, your brain recognizes the pattern. It has been here before. It knows what to do next.

A safe environment can also include patient conversation partners, tutors who prioritize flow over correction, or even structured prompts that limit the scope of what you need to say. What matters is that you experience repeated cycles of attempt, disruption, and continuation. Anxiety loses power when it no longer feels exceptional. When freezing becomes just another moment you know how to handle, it stops dominating your attention.

Recovery phrases are the bridge across these moments. They are not apologies. Apologizing reinforces the idea that something has gone wrong. Recovery phrases acknowledge difficulty without judgment and keep the interaction alive. When everything disappears mid-sentence, the worst move is to retreat into silence or switch languages immediately. The better move is to narrate the gap briefly and then continue with what you have. This transforms a breakdown into a transition.

At first, using recovery phrases may feel like admitting weakness. In practice, it does the opposite. It signals composure. Native speakers do this constantly without thinking about it. They hesitate, restart, rephrase, and fill space while searching for words. The difference is that they do it without shame. By adopting the same behavior early, you normalize the experience for yourself. Anxiety loses its edge when it no longer feels like exposure.

Anxiety-proofing your brain is not about becoming calm before you speak. It is about learning that you can speak while not calm and still be understood. Each successful recovery weakens the freeze response slightly. Over time, your threshold shifts. Situations that once triggered shutdown begin to feel manageable. Not because you know everything you might need to say, but because you trust your ability to navigate uncertainty in real time.

1.3 Your Spanish Identity

Beyond anxiety, there is a quieter obstacle that shapes how you speak: identity. When you speak your native language, you are not consciously performing who you are. You simply are. In a second language, that automatic sense of self often disappears. Many learners report feeling smaller, flatter, or less intelligent when speaking Spanish. This is not because Spanish diminishes them, but because their identity in the language is underdeveloped. They have words, but no voice yet.

Creating a Spanish identity is not about pretending to be someone else. It is about choosing a consistent way of showing up that reduces self-consciousness. When identity is vague, every sentence feels like a personal exposure. When identity is defined, speech becomes an expression of a role you are inhabiting. Actors do not feel embarrassed delivering lines on stage because the character carries the risk, not the person. A Spanish persona works the same way.

This persona can be subtle. It might simply be a slightly more expressive, slightly more forgiving version of yourself. Or it might be deliberately different: more playful, more formal, more relaxed. What matters is that it is chosen. Choice creates distance. Distance reduces emotional load. When you step into your Spanish persona, mistakes feel less like reflections of your worth and more like attributes of the role.

Tone is the backbone of this identity. Choosing whether your Spanish voice is friendly, professional, humorous, or calm has immediate practical effects. Tone determines vocabulary. A friendly tone relies on warmth, repetition, and simple connectors. A professional tone leans on clarity, structure, and neutral phrasing. A humorous tone accepts exaggeration and risk. When tone is undefined, you hesitate because you are trying to be everything at once. When tone is chosen, decisions become easier.

Many learners struggle because they unconsciously aim for a tone that is too complex for their current level. They want to sound clever, nuanced, or subtle before they have built fluency. This mismatch creates frustration. By selecting a tone that aligns with simplicity, you give yourself permission to reuse phrases, repeat structures, and rely on rhythm rather than novelty. Fluency thrives on reuse. Identity gives reuse legitimacy.

This is where a one-page voice guide becomes useful. Not as a formal document, but as a mental anchor. Your voice guide is a small collection of phrases, openings, and reactions that feel natural to you and that you will reuse frequently. These phrases form the skeleton of your speech. They appear again and again, slightly modified, across conversations. Far from limiting you, this repetition frees cognitive space. You no longer have to invent how to start or respond; you only have to adjust.

A voice guide also reinforces continuity. When you hear yourself using the same expressions across contexts, your Spanish starts to feel coherent. You recognize your own voice in the language. This recognition builds ownership. Spanish is no longer something you borrow for specific situations; it is something you inhabit. Identity solidifies not through variety, but through consistency.

Importantly, your Spanish identity is allowed to evolve. The first version is not permanent. In the early stages, its purpose is protective. It reduces exposure and supports participation. As your skills grow, the persona can expand. You may add nuance, humor, or assertiveness. But this expansion works only if there is a stable core underneath. Without that core, every attempt at expression feels experimental and draining.

Identity also interacts with confidence in a feedback loop. When you know who you are in Spanish, you speak more freely. When you speak more freely, your identity strengthens. This loop is fragile at the beginning and must be supported deliberately. That is why defining your tone and your go-to phrases early is not cosmetic. It is structural. It turns Spanish from a test of ability into a medium of expression.

Ultimately, building a Spanish identity is about reclaiming agency. Instead of asking, "Am I good enough to speak?" the question becomes, "How would someone like me say this?" That shift is profound. It moves the focus from evaluation to expression. And expression, even in simple forms, is what keeps the confidence engine running.

When anxiety is managed and identity is anchored, speaking stops feeling like an act of courage every single time. Courage is still there, but it is quieter. It shows up as consistency rather than adrenaline. You speak not because you are fearless, but because speaking is now aligned with who you are becoming in the language. And that alignment is what allows progress to compound.

Chapter 2 — Pronunciation That Makes You Instantly Understandable

2.1 The 10 Sounds That Matter Most

Most people imagine pronunciation as a kind of cosmetic polish, something you work on later, once you "know the language." That belief quietly sabotages clarity from the very beginning. Pronunciation is not decoration. It is infrastructure. If the sounds coming out of your mouth do not match what the listener's brain expects, comprehension slows down or breaks entirely, no matter how correct your grammar is. The good news is that you do not need a perfect accent, and you certainly do not need to sound native. You need intelligibility. And intelligibility in Spanish is surprisingly cheap. A small number of sound adjustments produce a disproportionate jump in how easily you are understood.

Spanish is acoustically forgiving. Its sound system is smaller and more regular than English, and that regularity works in your favor. The problem is that most learners import English habits without realizing it. English allows vague vowels, swallowed syllables, and elastic stress. Spanish does not. When English speakers struggle to be understood, it is rarely because they chose the wrong word. It is because the word they chose was reshaped by English muscle memory until it became something else entirely.

If you could only fix one thing in your pronunciation, it would be vowel purity. Spanish vowels are stable, short, and consistent. Each vowel has one main sound, and it does not slide. English vowels, by contrast, are slippery. They often begin in one position and glide into another, especially in stressed syllables. This glide is so automatic that most English speakers cannot hear it in themselves. In Spanish, that glide creates confusion. What sounds like a small variation to you can register as a different vowel or even a different word to the listener.

When you pronounce Spanish vowels cleanly, something immediate happens. Your speech becomes easier to parse. Native speakers stop leaning forward or narrowing their eyes. You may still make grammatical errors, but the listener no longer has to work to identify the word itself. This is why vowel purity is the single biggest clarity upgrade available. It affects every word you say, not just a few tricky ones.

Training this does not require musical talent or a special ear. It requires restraint. You are not trying to add sound; you are trying to remove movement. The vowel should feel almost flat, almost minimal, as if you are placing it and letting it go rather than shaping it dramatically. At first, this may feel unnatural or even dull. That sensation is a sign you are doing it right. Spanish vowels do not perform. They arrive and exit cleanly.

The next sounds that intimidate learners are the infamous "r" and "rr." They have acquired an almost mythical status, as if mastering them were a rite of passage. This drama is unnecessary and counterproductive. The truth is simpler. The Spanish single "r" and double "rr" are not exotic sounds; they are timing problems. They are not about force, but about contact.

The single "r" in Spanish is not the English "r" softened or rolled. It is a quick tap of the tongue against the ridge behind the teeth. If you already pronounce the "tt" sound in the middle of "butter" in American English, you are closer than you think. That soft, quick tap is essentially the Spanish single "r." You are not holding it. You are touching and releasing. Many learners overthink this and tense up, which makes the sound harder, not easier.

The double "rr" is simply that tap repeated rapidly. It is not produced by pushing air harder, and it is not achieved by straining the throat. In fact, tension is the enemy here. The tongue needs to be relaxed enough to vibrate. Practical drills that work focus on rhythm, not effort. You are teaching your tongue to bounce, not to fight. When people "suffer" with the rolled "r," it is usually because they are trying to dominate the sound instead of allowing it.

Importantly, imperfect "r" sounds rarely block understanding. A slightly weak roll is almost always preferable to an English-style "r" creeping in. The listener's brain can adjust to a soft or inconsistent roll far more easily than to a sound that belongs to a different language entirely. Clarity comes from being in the right neighborhood, not from hitting the exact house.

Beyond vowels and "r" sounds, the most damaging pronunciation issues come from predictable English-to-Spanish traps. These traps are dangerous because they feel natural. You do not hear them as mistakes; you hear them as normal speech. One common trap is vowel reduction. In English, unstressed vowels often collapse into a neutral sound. In Spanish, they do not. Every vowel is pronounced, even in fast speech. When you reduce vowels in Spanish, words lose their shape. The listener hears a blur where they expect structure.

Another trap is final consonant distortion. English allows consonants at the end of words to fade or soften. Spanish expects them to be clear. When final consonants disappear, words sound unfinished. This is especially noticeable with "d," "s," and "n." You do not need to exaggerate them, but you do need to complete them. Think of finishing the word rather than trailing off.

Stress placement is another silent culprit. Spanish stress is more predictable than English, and when it shifts incorrectly, intelligibility suffers. Even if every sound is technically correct, stress in the wrong place can slow comprehension. The listener's brain momentarily searches for a different word, and that delay adds up over a sentence. You do not need to memorize stress rules obsessively, but you do need to notice patterns and respect them. Consistent stress is part of what gives Spanish its rhythm.

There is also the issue of consonants that look familiar but behave differently. The Spanish "b" and "v," for example, are not distinguished the way they are in English. Treating them as separate sounds adds unnecessary complexity and can make your speech sound hesitant. The Spanish "d" between vowels is softer than its English counterpart, and forcing it too hard creates a foreign edge. These details matter not because they must be perfect, but because they accumulate. Each small adjustment reduces friction.

What ties all of this together is a shift in goal. You are not trying to sound impressive. You are trying to be easy to understand. Ease is the metric. If a native speaker can relax while listening to you, you are succeeding. This reframing removes enormous pressure. Instead of chasing an accent, you focus on reducing confusion. Instead of performing, you prioritize transmission.

Pronunciation improves fastest when it is connected to meaning, not isolated drills. Saying sounds in a vacuum has limited value. Saying them inside words you actually use is far more effective. Every time you pronounce a familiar phrase clearly, you reinforce both the sound and the message. This is another reason the "10 sounds that matter most" approach works. You are not scattering your attention across every possible nuance. You are concentrating effort where it pays dividends immediately.

As you work on these sounds, something encouraging happens. People start understanding you sooner in your sentences. They stop asking you to repeat yourself. Conversations flow with less effort on both sides. This feedback loop builds confidence in a grounded way. You do not feel confident because you believe you sound good. You feel confident because communication works.

Pronunciation, handled this way, becomes an ally rather than an obstacle. It is no longer a source of self-consciousness, but a practical tool you can refine incrementally. You fix one sound, and suddenly dozens of words become clearer. You adjust one habit, and your entire speech feels more stable. This leverage is why pronunciation deserves early attention.

By focusing on the sounds that matter most, you avoid the trap of perfectionism and the opposite trap of neglect. You do not ignore pronunciation, and you do not obsess over it. You treat it as what it is: a high-impact system with a small number of critical components. When those components are in place, Spanish becomes not only easier to understand, but easier to speak. The words come out with less resistance. And that ease, more than any accent, is what makes people lean in and listen.

2.2 Rhythm Over Perfection

When people say someone "sounds fluent," they are rarely commenting on grammar. What they are responding to is rhythm. Spanish has a musical logic that is fundamentally different from English, and once you align with it, intelligibility increases almost automatically. This is why rhythm matters more than perfect sounds. You can mispronounce a consonant and still be understood, but if your timing fights the language, even correct sounds feel foreign.

English is built on stress spikes. Some syllables are strong, others are reduced, and the contrast between them carries meaning. This creates a jagged rhythm, full of rises and drops. Spanish works differently. Its rhythm is smoother, more even, with syllables that take up roughly equal time. Instead of jumping from peak to valley, Spanish moves forward in a steady current. When English speakers bring stress spikes into Spanish, the result feels choppy. Words arrive out of balance, and the listener has to work harder to track them.

Understanding this changes how you speak. You stop trying to emphasize "important" words the way you would in English. Instead, you let the sentence flow, trusting that clarity will come from consistency rather than contrast. This does not mean Spanish is monotone. It has melody and intonation, but the melody rides on evenly timed syllables. Once you feel this, speaking becomes less effortful. You are no longer wrestling the language into your native rhythm.

One of the fastest ways to feel this difference is to pay attention to how Spanish speakers handle short, functional words. In English, these words often shrink or disappear acoustically. In Spanish, they stay present. Articles, prepositions, and connectors are pronounced clearly and linked smoothly to surrounding words. This linking is a major contributor to perceived fluency.

When words connect, speech sounds continuous rather than assembled piece by piece.

Linking does not require advanced grammar. In fact, simple grammar benefits the most. When you connect words naturally, even basic sentences sound fluid. The listener's brain receives a continuous stream instead of isolated blocks. This continuity creates the impression of confidence. Pauses still happen, but they feel intentional rather than hesitant.

Many learners pause between every word, as if each one must be placed carefully. This habit often comes from reading-based learning, where words appear visually separate. Spoken Spanish does not behave that way. Words lean into each other. Final sounds flow into initial sounds. Vowels meet vowels without a break. When you allow this to happen, you reduce the number of decisions you have to make while speaking. The sentence carries you forward.

This is where "mouth muscle training" becomes relevant. Pronunciation is not just an auditory skill; it is physical. Your mouth has learned certain movement patterns from your native language, and Spanish asks for different ones. Training these movements does not require long sessions. Short, focused routines repeated daily produce faster change because they target coordination, not knowledge.

A five-minute routine is enough if it is intentional. The goal is not to repeat sounds mechanically, but to experience smoothness. You want to feel how syllables connect without tension. At first, this may feel exaggerated, as if you are over-articulating. That sensation fades as the movements become familiar. Over time, your mouth stops defaulting to English patterns and begins to anticipate Spanish ones.

These routines work best when they are tied to rhythm rather than isolated sounds. Speaking full phrases at a steady pace trains timing more effectively than drilling individual consonants. You are teaching your mouth how to move through Spanish, not how to pose for it. Improvement shows up not as dramatic change, but as reduced effort. Speaking feels lighter. You finish sentences without running out of breath or momentum.

The most important shift in this phase is letting go of self-monitoring while speaking. If you try to correct every sound as it comes out, rhythm collapses. Fluency requires trust. You practice deliberately, and then you let go during use. Rhythm is maintained by flow, not by control. When you allow yourself to ride the sentence instead of managing it, Spanish starts to sound like Spanish.

2.3 Listening Like a Musician

Clear pronunciation is only half of intelligibility. The other half is listening. Not listening for meaning alone, but listening for structure. Many learners listen for words they recognize, treating speech as a string of items to be identified. This approach breaks down at natural speed. Spanish, like music, must be heard in units. Syllables, not words, are the building blocks.

Listening like a musician means focusing on timing and segmentation rather than translation. When musicians hear a melody, they do not analyze each note individually. They perceive patterns, phrasing, and rhythm. Language works the same way. Native speakers do not hear sentences as lists of words; they hear them as flowing shapes. Training yourself to hear syllables helps you access that shape.

Segmentation practice is the art of dividing the stream of sound into manageable units. At first, Spanish may sound fast and indistinct, not because it is faster, but because your brain does not yet know where one syllable ends and the next begins. By listening specifically for syllable boundaries, you train your brain to organize the sound. This organization makes everything else easier. Words emerge naturally once the rhythm is clear.

This kind of listening requires patience. You may understand less meaning initially because your attention is on sound. That is normal. You are building a foundation. Over time, meaning and sound reintegrate, and comprehension improves more quickly than it would have otherwise. This is why advanced listeners often say they are not translating at all. They are responding to patterns they recognize.

Shadowing is one of the most effective tools for developing this skill, but it must be used intelligently. Blind copying leads to mimicry without understanding. Effective shadowing is selective. You are not trying to replicate every detail. You are listening for rhythm, stress, and linkage. You let go of exact pitch and personal voice. Your goal is not to become the speaker, but to internalize the movement of their speech.

When shadowing, it is helpful to ignore elements that are idiosyncratic. Individual accents, emotional inflections, and regional quirks are not priorities at this stage. What matters is the underlying timing. How long syllables last. How words connect. Where pauses occur naturally. By focusing on these features, you avoid copying habits that may not serve your own clarity.

Recording yourself is where listening and speaking converge. Many learners avoid this because it feels uncomfortable. That discomfort is informative. When you listen back, you hear the gap between intention and execution. This gap is not a verdict; it is a map. It shows you where clarity is lost and where it holds.

A clarity checklist helps structure this process. You are not judging your accent. You are asking practical questions. Are syllables even, or do some collapse? Do words connect smoothly, or are there frequent breaks? Is the rhythm steady, or does it lurch? Are vowels consistent? These questions direct your attention to actionable elements. Improvement follows attention.

Listening to yourself also builds empathy for your listeners. You experience your speech as they do, without the internal context of what you meant to say. This perspective is invaluable. It trains you to anticipate confusion and adjust proactively. Over time, this feedback loop becomes internal. You sense when clarity drops and correct in real time.

Listening like a musician ultimately changes your relationship with Spanish. The language stops feeling like a puzzle to be solved and starts feeling like a flow to join. You become sensitive to its cadence. You notice when something sounds off, even if you cannot explain why yet. That sensitivity guides practice more effectively than rules.

As rhythm stabilizes and listening sharpens, pronunciation stops being a separate task. It integrates into communication. You are no longer "working on your accent." You are refining how you move through sound. This refinement accumulates quietly. One day, you realize people interrupt you less, ask you to repeat yourself less, and respond more naturally. Intelligibility has increased, not because you chased perfection, but because you aligned with the music of the language.

That alignment is the real goal of this chapter. When rhythm leads and listening supports, Spanish becomes cooperative. It meets you halfway. And in that cooperation, confidence grows—not from sounding flawless, but from being understood without effort.

Chapter 3 — The Core Sentence Patterns That Power Real Conversation

3.1 The 12 "Spine" Structures

If you listen closely to real conversations, you begin to notice something counterintuitive. People do not speak in an endless variety of sentence types. They circle around the same structures again and again, adjusting them slightly to fit the moment. These structures form the spine of everyday communication. Vocabulary changes, details shift, but the underlying frames stay remarkably stable. This is why some learners with limited vocabulary sound fluent, while others with thousands of words still hesitate. Fluency is not about how much you know. It is about how reliably you can assemble meaning under pressure.

The idea of "spine" structures reframes how you approach Spanish. Instead of collecting phrases and hoping they stick, you focus on mastering a small set of patterns that can carry almost any idea you need in daily life. Once these patterns are automatic, your brain no longer has to invent a sentence from scratch. It fills in slots. This reduces cognitive load and frees attention for listening, reacting, and adjusting. Conversation stops feeling like a puzzle and starts feeling like movement.

Among all sentence patterns, the most powerful engine in Spanish is built around expressions of intention, ability, obligation, and possession. "I want," "I need," "I can," and "I have to" appear constantly in real speech. They are not dramatic or sophisticated, but they are decisive. They allow you to direct action, express limits, negotiate plans, and assert preferences. Without them, you are reduced to reacting rather than initiating.

These structures work because they sit at the intersection of meaning and action. When you say what you want, need, can do, or must do, you are shaping the conversation. You are not merely answering questions; you are setting direction. This is why mastering these forms early has such a disproportionate impact on confidence. You move from passive participation to active presence.

What matters here is not memorizing conjugation charts, but internalizing the rhythm and feel of these frames. In real conversation, they tend to appear in short, efficient bursts. You do not need to embellish them. In fact, over-embellishment often makes them sound unnatural. The strength of these structures lies in their simplicity. They are designed to be said quickly and frequently.

Once these engines are in place, questions become the next layer of the spine. Many learners treat questions as special constructions that require careful planning. In reality, conversational questions are often built by lightly reshaping statements. The same core structures reappear, but with a shift in tone or order. This reuse is what keeps conversations moving. You ask, you answer, you follow up, all within a familiar framework.

Effective question frames do not aim for grammatical perfection. They aim for momentum. A good question opens space for the other person to speak without derailing the interaction. It signals interest and keeps the exchange alive. When you rely on a small set of question frames, you stop searching for "the right way" to ask something and start focusing on what you want to know.

This approach also reduces the fear of interrupting or sounding rude. When your questions are built on natural frames, they blend into the conversation. They feel like extensions rather than interruptions. This is particularly important in Spanish, where conversational overlap and responsiveness are common. Hesitation can be misread as disengagement. Simple, timely questions prevent that gap.

Opinion frames complete the spine. Expressing opinions is where many learners freeze, not because they lack ideas, but because they are unsure how to package them. Textbooks often teach elaborate opinion phrases that sound stiff in real life. Native speech tends to rely on lighter, more flexible frames. Opinions are often introduced tentatively, softened, or framed as personal perspectives rather than absolute statements.

These frames allow you to participate without overcommitting. You can agree partially, express uncertainty, or adjust your stance as the conversation evolves. This flexibility is crucial for sounding natural. Conversation is not a debate stage; it is a collaborative space. Opinion frames help you contribute while staying aligned with the flow.

What unites all twelve spine structures is their adaptability. Each one can host a wide range of vocabulary and contexts. You can talk about work, plans, feelings, or logistics using the same underlying patterns. This reuse creates a sense of coherence in your speech. Listeners begin to recognize your rhythm. They anticipate how your sentences unfold. That anticipation makes comprehension easier.

Another advantage of spine structures is that they are resilient under stress. When anxiety rises, complex constructions collapse. Simple, well-practiced frames survive. This is why learners often revert to basic sentences under pressure. Instead of fighting that tendency, you harness it. You deliberately train the structures that will still be available when your cognitive bandwidth is reduced.

As you practice these patterns, something subtle changes in how you listen. You start recognizing the same structures in others' speech. Conversations become more predictable, not in a boring way, but in a supportive one. You know where the sentence is going. You can jump in at the right moment. This shared structure creates rapport.

Importantly, mastering spine structures does not mean limiting expression. On the contrary, it creates freedom. When the structure is stable, you can play with tone, emphasis, and detail. You can be direct or polite, firm or tentative, without reinventing the sentence. Structure holds the shape while meaning moves inside it.

There is also an identity shift that comes with this mastery. You stop feeling like someone who is assembling language piece by piece and start feeling like someone who speaks. The difference is not knowledge, but automation. The sentences come out with less friction. You finish them more often. You start more conversations instead of waiting to be addressed.

The idea that "most daily conversations run on a small set of reusable structures" is not a simplification. It is an observation grounded in how language is actually used. People value clarity, speed, and connection more than novelty. By aligning your practice with this reality, you accelerate progress and reduce frustration.

This chapter is not about learning twelve things and moving on. It is about installing a framework that everything else will attach to. Vocabulary will grow. Grammar will refine itself. But without a spine, those elements float without support. With it, they lock into place.

By focusing on these core sentence patterns, you give your Spanish a backbone. You can stand upright in conversation, initiate, respond, and express yourself without constantly bracing for collapse. Fluency, in this sense, is not a distant goal. It is the experience of having reliable structures beneath your words. And once those structures are in place, real conversation stops being something you prepare for and becomes something you participate in naturally.

3.2 Building Blocks: Expand Without Getting Lost

Once you have a reliable set of core sentence patterns, the next challenge is expansion. This is where many learners stall. They can say a basic idea clearly, but the moment they try to add detail, the sentence collapses. They lose the verb, forget the structure, or abandon the thought halfway through. This is not a lack of ability. It is a design problem. The sentence was never built to carry extra weight.

Expansion in Spanish does not require rebuilding your sentence from the ground up. In fact, the most fluent speakers rarely do that. They add information in layers, almost as an afterthought, without disturbing the core. Understanding this changes how you speak. Instead of aiming for a perfect, fully formed sentence from the beginning, you start with a solid base and then attach meaning as it becomes available.

Time, place, and reason are the most common additions in daily speech. They answer natural follow-up questions and make your message feel complete. The key is that these elements can usually be added at the edges of a sentence. You do not need to interrupt the engine. You simply extend it. This keeps cognitive load low. Your brain is not managing multiple changes at once. It is continuing forward and adding context along the way.

Think of the sentence as a train. The engine is your core structure. Additional information is added as cars behind it. You do not stop the train to rearrange the engine. You keep moving and attach. This mental image matters because it mirrors how real conversation unfolds. Speakers rarely plan everything in advance. They speak, notice what is missing, and add it.

Time expressions often come first in expansion practice because they are concrete and flexible. You can say when something happens before or after the main idea, and both are acceptable. Place works the same way. You can locate an action without modifying its core. Reason is slightly more complex, but it follows the same principle. You do not justify everything upfront. You state, then explain.

This is where the "because ladder" becomes useful. Many learners believe that giving reasons requires long, complex sentences. In reality, explanations often start small. You give a simple reason, and if needed, you add another layer. This ladder approach keeps your speech fluent because you are never overcommitting. You explain just enough, then stop or continue based on the listener's response.

Simple explanations sound natural because they match conversational expectations. People do not expect dissertations in daily speech. They expect clarity. When you provide a brief reason, you show cooperation. If more detail is needed, the conversation will invite it. By using the because ladder, you align with this rhythm. You are not dumping information; you are responding.

Connectors are the tools that make this layering smooth. Words like pero, entonces, aunque, and por eso do more than link clauses. They signal relationships. They tell the listener how to interpret what comes next. Used naturally, they create flow even when the language itself is simple.

The mistake many learners make with connectors is treating them as decorations. They sprinkle them in without adjusting tone or timing. In natural speech, connectors often appear at moments of transition, sometimes with a brief pause. They act like hinges. When you respect that function, your sentences feel intentional rather than assembled.

Pero introduces contrast. It allows you to adjust or soften what you just said. Entonces moves the conversation forward, showing consequence or progression. Aunque introduces nuance without confrontation. Por eso closes a loop, linking cause and result. These connectors are powerful because they work with basic sentences. You do not need advanced grammar to use them effectively. You need awareness.

By practicing expansion through building blocks, you avoid the trap of overengineering. You keep your sentences alive and adaptable. Fluency grows not from complexity, but from the ability to add and adjust without freezing.

3.3 The Flow Method: From Basic to Natural

Knowing how to expand a sentence is only half the story. The other half is knowing how to do it without sounding robotic. Many learners reach a stage where their Spanish is correct but stiff. The sentences are complete, but they feel written, not spoken. This is where the flow method comes in.

Flow is not about adding sophistication. It is about softening edges. Natural speech is full of small adjustments that make sentences sound lived-in rather than assembled. These adjustments do not change meaning; they change texture. When you learn to apply them, your Spanish begins to breathe.

The first step in the flow method is recognizing that robotic speech often comes from overprecision. You try to say exactly what you would say in your native language, word for word. This creates two problems. First, it overloads your sentence with structure that Spanish does not need. Second, it pulls you into literal translation traps. You preserve meaning, but you distort form.

Avoiding these traps does not mean abandoning your meaning. It means expressing it in a way Spanish naturally allows. This often involves choosing simpler phrasing and letting context do some of the work. Native speakers rely heavily on shared understanding. They do not spell everything out. When you try to replicate every nuance explicitly, your speech becomes heavy.

The flow method encourages you to start simple and then upgrade gradually. You begin with a basic sentence that communicates the core idea. Then you add one element that makes it sound more conversational. This might be a connector, a softener, or a timing adjustment. You are not rewriting the sentence; you are tuning it.

This tuning process works best when practiced in levels. At the first level, you aim for clarity only. You say the sentence in its simplest workable form. At the second level, you expand it slightly, adding time, reason, or connection. At the third level, you adjust for naturalness, introducing rhythm and tone. Each level builds on the previous one. You never skip steps.

This layered practice mirrors how fluency develops. You do not jump from basic to advanced in one move. You evolve through manageable transitions. By practicing all three levels, you teach your brain that natural speech is not a separate skill. It is an extension of what you already know.

Another key aspect of flow is learning when not to upgrade. Not every sentence needs polish. In fact, constant upgrading can slow you down. Flow includes knowing when to stay simple. Short, direct sentences are a feature of spoken Spanish, not a flaw. When you respect that, your speech gains credibility.

Literal translation traps often appear when you try to express abstract ideas too early. The flow method suggests postponing abstraction. You express concrete ideas first, then add interpretation if needed. This keeps you anchored. You are less likely to reach for structures that do not belong.

Over time, these practices change how you think while speaking. You stop planning entire sentences in advance. You start speaking in segments, listening to yourself, and adjusting in real time. This is the essence of conversational flow. You are not delivering a monologue. You are participating in a dynamic exchange.

The three-level practice also builds resilience. If you lose your thread, you can always drop back to a simpler level without stopping. You do not panic. You adapt. This flexibility is what allows conversations to continue even when your language resources are stretched.

As flow develops, you may notice something subtle. You begin to recognize when your own sentences sound natural before anyone reacts. This internal feedback is a sign that your Spanish identity is consolidating. You are no longer guessing. You are sensing.

Ultimately, the flow method is about trust. Trusting that simplicity is enough. Trusting that meaning can emerge through interaction. Trusting that you do not need to control every word. When you combine strong core structures with flexible expansion and gentle upgrading, real conversation becomes sustainable.

By mastering these building blocks and practicing flow deliberately, you turn Spanish into a system you can grow inside without getting lost. Each sentence supports the next. Each adjustment builds confidence. Fluency stops being a distant concept and becomes a daily experience, constructed one stable, adaptable sentence at a time.

Chapter 4 — Vocabulary That Sticks: Learn Words the Way Your Brain Likes

4.1 High-Return Vocabulary (Not Random Word Hoarding)

Most people think they need more vocabulary. What they actually need is better vocabulary decisions. Word hoarding feels productive because it creates the illusion of progress. You can count words. You can highlight them. You can check them off a list. The problem is that your brain does not work like a warehouse. It works like a network. Words that are not connected to use, emotion, or repetition fade quickly, no matter how many times you looked at them on a page.

Memory improves when words are tied to something that matters. Context gives them shape. Emotion gives them weight. Use gives them permanence. This is why you can remember lines from a song you love without effort but struggle to recall a word you studied ten times yesterday. The difference is not intelligence or discipline. It is relevance.

High-return vocabulary is vocabulary that earns its place. These are words that appear frequently, combine easily with other words, and show up in situations you actually encounter. When you prioritize them, your Spanish begins to feel functional early. You stop waiting to "know enough" and start noticing that you can already express most of what you need.

The first layer of high-return vocabulary is what could be called the daily life set. These are verbs and nouns that appear constantly, regardless of topic. They describe basic actions, states, and needs. They are not exciting, but they are foundational. Without them, everything else floats. With them, even limited language becomes useful.

What makes this set powerful is not just frequency, but flexibility. These words combine naturally with many sentence structures. They appear in past, present, and future contexts. They anchor your speech. When learners struggle to speak, it is often because they are missing these anchors and trying to compensate with more specific but less adaptable words.

The daily life set also benefits from repetition in natural contexts. You encounter these words everywhere: conversations, signs, messages, instructions. Each encounter reinforces them. When you deliberately focus on this set, you amplify that reinforcement. The words stop being "new." They become familiar companions.

The second layer is the conversation set. This is where many courses fall short. They teach nouns and verbs but neglect the small words that actually make conversation feel human. Reactions, fillers, and softeners do not carry heavy meaning, but they carry social signal. They show engagement, hesitation, agreement, surprise, or doubt. Without them, your speech may be correct but feels abrupt or mechanical.

These words act as lubricant. They smooth transitions. They buy you time. They signal that you are listening, not just waiting to speak. Native speakers rely on them constantly, often without noticing. When you add them to your active vocabulary, conversations become less stressful because you are no longer forced to respond with full, polished sentences every time.

The conversation set is also emotionally powerful. These words are tied to feeling states. When you learn them, you are not just learning language; you are learning how Spanish expresses presence. This emotional link makes them easier to remember. You recall them because you recall the feeling they accompany.

The third layer is the personal set, and it is the most overlooked. These are words connected to your actual life: your work, your hobbies, your routines, your interests. Generic vocabulary lists cannot predict this set for you. It must be curated. The brain remembers what it uses to represent the self. When a word helps you talk about who you are or what you care about, it sticks.

This is why two learners at the same level can have very different vocabularies and both be fluent in their own way. They have invested in different personal sets. One can talk easily about work but struggles with small talk. Another navigates social situations smoothly but avoids professional topics. Neither is wrong. Fluency is not uniform. It is contextual.

When you build your personal set intentionally, vocabulary study stops feeling abstract. Each word has a job. You know when you will use it. You can imagine yourself using it. That mental simulation strengthens memory. The word is no longer a stranger; it has a role.

High-return vocabulary also reduces anxiety. When you know you have the words you need for your most common situations, you feel prepared. Preparation does not eliminate uncertainty, but it narrows it. You are not trying to be ready for every possible conversation. You are ready for the conversations you actually have.

Another benefit of focusing on high-return vocabulary is that it supports structure. Words are easier to remember when they fit into sentences you already use. This creates a virtuous cycle. Strong structures make vocabulary stick, and strong vocabulary reinforces structures. Random word hoarding breaks this cycle.

You collect words that do not attach to anything, and they drift away.

There is also a hidden cost to random accumulation: interference. When you learn many low-frequency or unrelated words at once, they compete in memory. Retrieval becomes slower. You hesitate more. This hesitation feeds the belief that you are "bad at vocabulary." In reality, the problem is selection, not capacity.

Learning words the way your brain likes means respecting its preferences. It prefers patterns over lists, relevance over volume, and use over exposure. It wants to solve problems, not store data. When you give it words that solve immediate communicative problems, it rewards you with recall.

This approach also changes how you review. Instead of scanning long lists, you revisit words in action. You recall them while speaking, writing short messages, or thinking through scenarios. Each retrieval strengthens the neural pathway. Passive recognition is replaced by active use.

High-return vocabulary is not about minimalism for its own sake. It is about leverage. A small, well-chosen set of words can generate an outsized range of expression. As your fluency grows, you will naturally add more. But those additions will attach to a strong foundation instead of floating aimlessly.

By resisting the urge to hoard and choosing words that earn their place, you align your learning with how memory actually works. Vocabulary stops being something you chase and starts being something you inhabit. Words arrive when you need them, not because you forced them in, but because you gave them a reason to stay.

This is the shift that makes vocabulary stick. Not effort alone, but alignment. When you learn words the way your brain likes,

Spanish stops feeling like a list you must memorize and becomes a language you can actually live in.

4.2 Context-Based Acquisition

Your brain does not store words as isolated entries. It stores experiences. When you try to learn vocabulary as if it were a list of interchangeable labels, you work against that reality. Context-based acquisition reverses the process. Instead of asking your brain to remember a word and then figure out how to use it later, you introduce the word already embedded in meaning. The brain recognizes this as useful information and treats it differently. It keeps it accessible.

Micro-stories are one of the simplest and most effective ways to do this. A micro-story is not a creative writing exercise. It is a small, concrete situation that gives a word a role. Even a single sentence can be enough if it describes a clear action or feeling. The power of a micro-story comes from specificity. When a word is linked to a moment, your brain remembers the moment and retrieves the word along with it.

This works because memory evolved to support survival, not exams. Situations mattered. Abstract labels did not. When you learn a word through a tiny narrative, you activate multiple pathways at once: language, imagery, and emotion. You are no longer asking your brain to store a symbol. You are asking it to store a scene.

The scene does not need to be dramatic. In fact, ordinary scenes work best because they resemble real life. Ordering coffee, missing a bus, finishing a task late, feeling tired at the end of the day. These are experiences your brain already knows. When a Spanish word enters one of these frames, it feels familiar faster. The word stops being foreign and starts behaving like something you have lived.

Micro-stories also reduce ambiguity. Many words have multiple meanings or subtle uses. Lists cannot capture that. Stories can.

When you encounter the word again in a similar context, recognition is immediate. When you encounter it in a different context, you have a reference point for comparison. Meaning becomes flexible instead of brittle.

Closely related to this is the idea of collocations, though you do not need linguistic terminology to benefit from it. Some words naturally belong together. They appear as pairs or clusters. Native speakers rarely assemble sentences word by word. They retrieve chunks. When you learn words in these natural groupings, fluency accelerates because retrieval becomes automatic.

Understanding collocations in plain terms means noticing patterns. Which verbs tend to appear with which nouns. Which adjectives feel natural with certain ideas. These combinations are not arbitrary. They reflect how the language organizes experience. When you respect these pairings, your speech sounds smoother, and you hesitate less because you are not making as many decisions.

Context-based learning highlights these pairings naturally. When you encounter words together in a story or a real situation, your brain links them. This link is stronger than any rule you could memorize. Over time, you develop an intuitive sense of what "sounds right," even before you can explain it. That intuition is a marker of real acquisition.

Visual hooks amplify this effect. When you attach a clear mental image to a word or phrase, recall speeds up dramatically. The image does not need to be elaborate. It needs to be distinct. The brain is excellent at remembering visuals, especially when they are slightly exaggerated or emotionally colored. A boring image fades. A vivid one sticks.

Emotional anchors deepen memory further. Emotion tells the brain that something matters. This does not mean you need intense feelings. Mild emotion is enough. Amusement, frustration, relief, curiosity. When a word is learned in a moment that carries feeling, it gains priority in memory. You remember it not because you forced repetition, but because it is tagged as relevant.

This is why personal relevance keeps resurfacing in effective language learning. Words connected to your life carry built-in emotion. They are not neutral. They represent parts of you. When you integrate new vocabulary into contexts that matter to you, forgetting becomes less likely. The word is no longer an abstract unit. It is a tool you have used.

4.3 A System That Prevents Forgetting

Learning words is only half the challenge. Keeping them accessible is the real test. Forgetting is not a personal failure; it is a natural process. Memory decays when information is not revisited. The question is not how to eliminate forgetting, but how to work with it intelligently.

Spaced repetition is often presented as a technical solution requiring apps and complex schedules. At its core, it is simpler. Information strengthens when it is recalled just as it is about to be forgotten. You do not need precision. You need consistency. A system you actually follow will outperform a perfect system you abandon.

A practical schedule respects your attention and your time. New words are revisited soon, then at increasing intervals. The exact timing matters less than the pattern. Early recall prevents loss. Later recall stabilizes memory. The key is that recall is active. You are not rereading. You are retrieving.

Active recall can happen without technology. In fact, removing apps often improves focus. You can test yourself by covering definitions, by recalling words during short pauses, or by prompting yourself with situations instead of translations. When you struggle to recall, that struggle is productive. It signals to the brain that the information is valuable.

Short, frequent recall sessions beat long, infrequent ones. Memory responds to rhythm. A few minutes of focused recall integrated into daily life builds resilience. You stop treating review as a separate task and start treating it as maintenance.

The "use it today" rule is the bridge between learning and speaking. Any new word you learn should be used within twenty-four hours. This rule changes behavior. You no longer learn words speculatively. You learn them with intention. You look for opportunities to deploy them. This turns vocabulary into action.

Using a word does not require a perfect sentence or a real conversation. You can speak it out loud to yourself, write a short message, or mentally rehearse a scenario. What matters is production. Production forces retrieval and integration. The word becomes part of your active system.

This rule also creates feedback. When you try to use a word and struggle, you learn something important. Maybe the word is less useful than you thought. Maybe you need its common partners. Maybe you misunderstood its nuance. This information guides refinement. Vocabulary study becomes responsive instead of rigid.

A system that prevents forgetting is not about discipline. It is about design. It aligns with how your brain prioritizes information. It rewards relevance, use, and timing. It minimizes waste by focusing effort where it pays off.

Over time, this system creates a sense of stability. Words stop slipping away unexpectedly. You trust your recall more. That trust reduces anxiety and frees attention for conversation. You are no longer mentally scanning for missing pieces. You are speaking with what you have.

Context-based acquisition and smart retention work together. Context makes words memorable. The system keeps them accessible. One without the other is incomplete. Together, they create vocabulary that sticks.

When words are learned in context, revisited strategically, and used quickly, they move from short-term awareness to long-term ownership. They become part of how you think in Spanish, not just what you know about it. This is when vocabulary stops feeling like something you manage and starts feeling like something you live.

By building a system that respects memory rather than fighting it, you give yourself an advantage that compounds. Each new word strengthens the network instead of burdening it. Forgetting slows. Confidence grows. And Spanish becomes not a collection of terms, but a language that responds when you reach for it.

Chapter 5 — Grammar Without Pain: The Minimum You Need to Speak Well

5.1 Present Tense Mastery for Real Life

Grammar has earned a bad reputation because it is often introduced as a system of rules to memorize rather than a set of tools to use. For many learners, grammar feels like a gatekeeper. Speak incorrectly and you are judged. Speak too slowly and you are invisible. This mindset turns grammar into a source of tension, when in reality it should function like a steering wheel. You do not need to understand every mechanical detail of a car to drive it. You need enough control to move forward, turn when necessary, and avoid crashing. Present tense grammar in Spanish works the same way.

The present tense is the engine of daily communication. Most of what you say about your life, your needs, your plans, and your opinions lives here. Even when you talk about the future or the past, you often anchor it in the present. Mastery in this context does not mean perfection. It means reliability. You can express basic actions clearly and consistently, without stopping to negotiate form every time you open your mouth.

The fastest way to reach that reliability is not by studying every verb, but by focusing on the ones that actually appear in your speech. A small group of high-frequency verbs carries an enormous amount of conversational weight. These verbs describe wanting, needing, having, being, going, doing, and saying. When they are stable, the rest of your language becomes easier to manage. When they are shaky, everything feels unstable.

What matters is not knowing their full conjugation tables, but recognizing how they behave in the present tense when you speak. In conversation, verbs tend to appear in predictable forms. You use them to talk about yourself, about others, and about general situations. When you internalize these patterns, you stop thinking in terms of rules and start thinking in terms of use.

Present tense mastery also reduces cognitive load. If you trust your verbs, you can focus on meaning instead of form. This trust is built through repetition in real contexts, not through abstract drills. Each time you successfully use a verb to achieve a communicative goal, you reinforce its pattern. Over time, the correct form feels obvious, not because you reasoned it out, but because you have experienced it repeatedly.

No discussion of Spanish present tense feels complete without addressing ser and estar. These two verbs are often framed as a nightmare, a conceptual puzzle that must be solved before you can speak. This framing creates unnecessary fear. In practice, native speakers use ser and estar automatically, guided by meaning rather than theory. You can approximate this behavior with a few practical shortcuts.

The most useful distinction is not permanent versus temporary, which is often misleading, but identification versus condition. Ser identifies what something is in a defining sense. Estar describes how something is in a given moment or situation. This mental split is easier to apply in real time. When you are naming, classifying, or defining, ser usually takes the lead. When you are describing a state, a feeling, or a location, estar tends to appear.

These shortcuts are not perfect, but they are functional. They cover the majority of everyday cases. Importantly, occasional misuse of ser and estar rarely blocks comprehension. Listeners may notice, but they almost always understand. This is a crucial point. Fear of getting them wrong often silences learners more than actual errors ever would. When you accept that approximation is enough, you free yourself to speak.

Another source of frustration in present tense grammar is sentence structure. Many common mistakes do not come from misunderstanding Spanish grammar, but from importing English structure directly. Word order, subject omission, and agreement behave differently in Spanish. When these differences are ignored, sentences may sound off or become harder to process.

One common issue is overusing subject pronouns. In English, the subject is almost always stated. In Spanish, it is often unnecessary because the verb already carries that information. When you repeat the subject unnecessarily, your speech becomes heavier and less natural. This does not usually block understanding, but it affects flow. Learning to trust the verb and drop the subject when it is clear makes your Spanish more efficient.

Agreement errors are another area where comprehension can suffer. Spanish relies more heavily on agreement than English. Adjectives and nouns must align. When they do not, the listener has to pause and reinterpret. You do not need to master every agreement rule immediately, but you do need to be aware of the most frequent patterns. Awareness prevents repeated errors from fossilizing.

Word order mistakes can also interfere with clarity. Spanish allows more flexibility than English, but that flexibility has boundaries. When key elements appear in unexpected positions, the listener's brain slows down. This is not about sounding formal or informal; it is about signaling relationships clearly. When you place elements where Spanish expects them, understanding becomes smoother.

Present tense mastery is therefore less about correctness and more about predictability. You want your listener to feel comfortable following your sentences. You want to reduce the moments where they have to guess what you mean. This comfort comes from stable verb use, reasonable ser and estar choices, and sentence structures that align with Spanish expectations.

It is important to remember that grammar exists to serve communication. When it blocks communication, something has gone wrong in how it is being used or taught. By focusing on the minimum you need to speak well, you avoid the paralysis that comes from overlearning. You do not need every tense, every exception, or every theoretical distinction. You need a functional present tense that allows you to express your life as it unfolds.

As you grow more comfortable, additional grammar will find its place naturally. It will attach to something you already use. This is how grammar becomes intuitive rather than oppressive. You are not memorizing rules in isolation. You are refining a system that is already working.

When grammar feels like a steering wheel, you stop staring at it and start looking at the road. You make small adjustments without thinking. You correct course when necessary. And most importantly, you keep moving. Present tense mastery gives you that movement. It anchors your Spanish in the now, where real conversations live, and gives you just enough control to drive with confidence.

5.2 Past and Future Without Overthinking

For many learners, the moment conversation drifts into the past or future is where confidence collapses. The present tense feels manageable, even comfortable, but as soon as you need to say what happened yesterday or what will happen next week, your mind fills with rules, tables, and warnings. This reaction is understandable. Past and future tenses are often taught as if they require total mastery before use. In reality, everyday speech relies on a much smaller toolkit than grammar books suggest.

Talking about the past does not begin with memorizing multiple tenses and their exceptions. It begins with anchoring time. When the listener knows when something happened, they become far more tolerant of imperfect grammar. Time markers do much of the work. Words that situate events in relation to now create a frame that the verb can sit inside. Once that frame is clear, communication succeeds even if the verb form is not elegant.

The simplest way to talk about yesterday and last week is to rely on one main past form and use it consistently. You do not need to distinguish between subtle shades of completion and description at the beginning. Native speakers may do this automatically, but learners can communicate effectively without that level of nuance. What matters is that your listener understands that the action is finished and placed in the past.

This approach removes panic because it removes choice. When you have one default way to speak about past events, you stop hesitating. Hesitation is often more damaging to fluency than inaccuracy. By choosing a simple strategy and applying it broadly, you keep the conversation moving. Movement builds confidence. Confidence allows refinement later.

Most everyday past talk involves recounting actions, not painting scenes. You talk about what you did, where you went, who you saw. These are discrete events. A single past tense handles them well enough. Even if you occasionally misuse a form that a textbook would flag, comprehension remains intact. Listeners fill in the gaps because the story is clear.

Future talk can be approached with the same philosophy. Instead of wrestling with the full future tense from the beginning, you can rely on a construction that mirrors how people plan in real life. Talking about intentions, plans, and near-future actions often uses a simple structure that feels almost present. This structure aligns with how the brain already thinks about the future: as something connected to now.

The distinction between using a periphrastic future and a simple future tense is often overstated in learning materials. In practice, the difference is less about grammar and more about perspective. When you are talking about plans you have already formed or actions you are about to take, the periphrastic structure feels natural. It signals intention rather than prediction. This makes it easier to use and easier to understand.

The simple future tense tends to appear when you are making predictions, expressing certainty, or speaking more formally. These contexts exist, but they are less common in casual conversation. By prioritizing the structure that covers the majority of real-life uses, you reduce complexity without sacrificing clarity.

Again, time markers play a critical role. Words that indicate when something will happen anchor your meaning. Tomorrow, next week, later, soon. These markers guide interpretation. Even if your verb choice is not textbook-perfect, the listener understands your intention. Time markers act like signposts. They tell the listener how to read the sentence.

Overthinking disappears when you stop trying to encode everything in the verb. Spanish, like all languages, distributes meaning across the sentence. Time is not carried by the verb alone. It is supported by context. When you use that context effectively, you free yourself from grammatical anxiety.

This approach to past and future is not about avoiding learning. It is about sequencing learning sensibly. You start with what allows you to communicate. Precision can come later, when it has something to attach to. Trying to master everything at once leads to paralysis. Mastering enough leads to momentum.

5.3 The Confidence Grammar Toolkit

Beyond tense, there are a few grammatical elements that disproportionately affect how confident and fluent you sound. These are not glamorous topics. They are often described as "small words" or minor details. In reality, they are structural glue. When used reasonably well, they make speech smoother and more natural. When ignored completely, they can cause confusion.

Gender and agreement fall into this category. Spanish marks gender more consistently than English, and this can feel overwhelming at first. The mistake many learners make is aiming for perfection too early. This creates stress and slows speech. The goal at this stage is not flawless agreement. It is accuracy sufficient for understanding.

Most gender errors do not block comprehension. Listeners are remarkably good at inferring meaning from context. However, repeated agreement mistakes in key places can create friction. The solution is not to memorize every rule, but to develop awareness of patterns. Certain endings recur frequently. When you notice and reuse them, your accuracy improves naturally.

Agreement becomes easier when it is tied to words you use often. High-frequency nouns and adjectives deserve extra attention because they appear repeatedly. Each time you get them right, you reinforce the pattern. Over time, these patterns become automatic. You stop thinking about them because your ear recognizes what fits.

Pronouns are another area where small improvements yield large gains. Words like me, te, lo, and le appear constantly in natural speech. They allow you to avoid repetition and sound more fluid. Many learners avoid them because they seem complicated. This avoidance keeps their speech heavier than necessary.

Understanding pronouns functionally rather than theoretically makes them accessible. You do not need to classify every pronoun or predict its position in complex sentences. You need to recognize what it replaces and why. When a pronoun stands in for something already mentioned, it lightens the sentence. It signals that you are tracking the conversation.

Using pronouns also changes rhythm. Sentences become shorter and more connected. This contributes to fluency more than perfect verb endings ever could. Even partial or inconsistent pronoun use improves flow. You do not need mastery to benefit.

The "good enough" rule ties all of this together. Grammar matters, but not all grammar matters equally. Some errors interfere with meaning. Others simply mark you as a learner. The art is knowing the difference. When you prioritize forms that support comprehension and flow, you allocate effort wisely.

Perfection matters when an error changes who did what to whom, or when it obscures time and intention. It matters less when the error is stylistic or redundant. Native speakers themselves are not perfectly consistent. They rely on context, repair, and shared understanding. You are allowed to do the same.

The confidence grammar toolkit is not a checklist. It is a mindset. You use grammar to support communication, not to audition for approval. You notice patterns. You refine gradually. You accept approximation as part of the process.

As you apply this toolkit, grammar stops feeling like a barrier and starts feeling like assistance. You make fewer mistakes that block meaning. You recover faster when you do. You trust yourself to keep speaking even when things are not perfect.

This trust is the real outcome of grammar without pain. When you stop fearing rules and start using them as guides, you reclaim energy for conversation. Past and future stop being danger zones. Small words become allies. And grammar takes its rightful place—not as a cage, but as a steering wheel that helps you move forward with confidence.

Chapter 6 — Conversation Control: Keep Talking Even When You're Stuck

6.1 The Survival Phrases That Make You Sound Fluent

The difference between someone who sounds fluent and someone who sounds stuck is rarely vocabulary size. It is control. Fluent speakers are not people who always know the right word; they are people who know what to do when they don't. They understand that conversation is not a test of knowledge but a dynamic process. Gaps are normal. Pauses are expected. What matters is whether the interaction continues to move forward.

Most learners experience getting stuck as a personal failure. A word disappears, a sentence collapses, and suddenly the entire conversation feels threatened. In that moment, many people retreat into silence, switch languages, or apologize repeatedly. These reactions break momentum. Native speakers, by contrast, treat gaps as minor inconveniences. They signal them, navigate around them, and keep going. Survival phrases are the tools that make this possible.

Survival phrases are not emergency measures you use only when things go wrong. They are part of normal speech. They buy time, clarify meaning, and share responsibility with the listener. When you use them naturally, you sound engaged and confident, even when your language is incomplete. The paradox is that admitting difficulty fluently makes you sound more fluent overall.

One of the most powerful survival tools is the ability to ask for a word without stopping the conversation. "How do you say…?" is often taught as a beginner phrase, but in real life it is a marker of competence. It shows that you are committed to expressing a specific idea and that you expect the interaction to support you. The key is not the phrase itself, but what you do next.

When learners ask for a word and then fall silent, waiting passively, momentum drops. Fluent speakers keep talking around the gap. They describe, gesture, paraphrase, or give examples. This does two things at once. It increases the chance that the listener will understand and provide the word, and it keeps the conversational rhythm alive. You are not halting progress; you are steering around an obstacle.

Follow-ups matter here. Instead of treating the missing word as a dead end, you treat it as a temporary placeholder. You continue with partial language, trusting that the meaning will land. This trust is audible. Listeners respond to it by leaning in rather than checking out. Conversation is cooperative by nature. When you show willingness to work through a gap, others meet you halfway.

Clarifying and confirming meaning is another area where survival phrases transform interaction. Many learners fear repetition because they associate it with confusion or weakness. In reality, repetition is a sign of control. Repeating what you think you heard, rephrasing it slightly, or checking understanding shows active listening. It signals confidence, not doubt.

Fluent speakers constantly adjust and confirm. They restate ideas, ask brief confirmation questions, and align their understanding with the other person's. This keeps conversations smooth and prevents misunderstandings from growing. When learners avoid clarification out of fear of appearing incompetent, they often end up more confused and less confident.

Repeating to confirm also gives you time. It slows the exchange just enough for your brain to catch up, without breaking flow. You are still speaking. You are still engaged. The conversation breathes. This is fundamentally different from freezing silently while searching for words internally.

Buying time naturally is an art that separates functional speakers from hesitant ones. Silence is not always bad, but unplanned silence often feels uncomfortable. Fillers and softeners exist to manage this space. In English, people use them constantly without thinking. Spanish has its own equivalents, and using them well signals conversational maturity.

The mistake many learners make is avoiding fillers entirely or overusing childish ones. They either speak in abrupt, clipped sentences or lean on sounds that feel inappropriate for adult conversation. The goal is balance. You want fillers that sound neutral and natural, not exaggerated or apologetic.

Time-buying phrases work best when they are paired with forward motion. You are not stalling; you are transitioning. You signal that you are thinking, adjusting, or preparing to add something. This keeps the listener oriented. They know something is coming. Anticipation replaces impatience.

Survival phrases also help manage emotional pressure. When you acknowledge difficulty out loud, you externalize it. The problem moves from inside your head into the shared space of the conversation. This reduces anxiety. You are no longer alone with the gap. You are working on it together.

Another overlooked benefit is identity reinforcement. When you handle gaps smoothly, you start seeing yourself as someone who can navigate conversation, not someone who must avoid it. Each successful recovery rewires expectation. The next time you get stuck, your nervous system remembers that you survived before. Confidence grows quietly through repetition of these moments.

It is important to note that survival phrases are not scripts to memorize and deploy mechanically. They are patterns to inhabit. You adapt them to your tone and personality. You make them yours. This personalization is what prevents them from sounding artificial. When a phrase aligns with how you naturally communicate, it becomes invisible. It blends into your speech.

Conversation control is not about dominating interaction. It is about maintaining continuity. You respect the other person's time and attention by keeping things moving. Even when your language is limited, your presence is steady. This steadiness is what people respond to.

Fluent speakers understand that meaning is negotiated, not delivered. Survival phrases are negotiation tools. They allow you to ask, adjust, and align in real time. They transform gaps from threats into opportunities for connection. When you use them, conversation feels resilient. It can bend without breaking.

As you practice these phrases, you will notice a shift. You stop dreading moments of uncertainty. You may even welcome them, because they give you a chance to practice control. Each gap becomes a small test you know how to pass. Not by knowing more words, but by staying in the interaction.

This is the essence of conversational fluency. Not completeness, but continuity. Not perfection, but recovery. When you master survival phrases, you are no longer dependent on ideal conditions to speak. You can function in real conversations, with real unpredictability. And that ability—to keep talking even when you're stuck—is what makes you sound fluent long before you actually are.

6.2 Repair Strategies (What to Do After a Mistake)

Mistakes are not interruptions to conversation; they are part of its texture. Fluent speakers make them constantly. They misspeak, restart, change direction mid-sentence, or choose a word that doesn't land. What separates them from hesitant speakers is not accuracy, but recovery. They know how to repair without collapsing the interaction. Repair is a skill, and like any skill, it can be trained deliberately.

The instinctive response after a mistake is often panic. Your attention turns inward. You replay the error, worry about how it sounded, and momentarily disconnect from the other person. This internal spiral does more damage than the mistake itself. Conversation is fragile not because of errors, but because of disengagement. Repair strategies exist to keep you oriented outward, toward meaning and connection.

Self-correction is one of the most misunderstood aspects of fluency. Many learners believe they must either correct every mistake immediately or avoid correction altogether. Both extremes are counterproductive. Overcorrection disrupts rhythm and draws unnecessary attention to form. Never correcting can allow confusion to accumulate. The balance lies in correcting lightly, only when it serves clarity.

Effective self-correction is brief and integrated. You do not stop to explain what went wrong. You simply replace the word or structure and continue. Native speakers do this instinctively. They correct themselves without apology, often without even pausing. This signals confidence. It tells the listener that the speaker is in control of their speech, even when adjusting it.

The key is timing. If the mistake affects meaning or could cause misunderstanding, a quick correction is helpful. If it is minor and the message is already clear, ignoring it is often the better choice. Conversation values momentum over precision. When you preserve flow, listeners stay engaged. When you interrupt flow for small errors, you risk losing attention.

Learning when to ignore errors is liberating. Most grammatical slips, pronunciation quirks, or agreement issues do not block comprehension. Listeners automatically compensate. When you stop treating every imperfection as an emergency, your speech becomes more relaxed. This relaxation improves performance more than correction ever could.

The emotional component of repair is just as important as the technical one. Many learners feel embarrassed after making a mistake and try to compensate by apologizing or retreating. These reactions shift the focus away from the topic and onto the error. They also place emotional burden on the listener, who must reassure you. Skilled speakers avoid this trap by treating errors as neutral events.

The "repair sandwich" is a useful mental model here. You briefly acknowledge the issue, fix it, and then continue forward. The acknowledgment does not have to be explicit. Often it is implied by the correction itself. The important part is that the continuation comes immediately. You do not linger. You move on as if the repair were a normal part of speech, which it is.

This approach keeps the conversation intact. The listener registers the correction and follows along without friction. Over time, using this strategy retrains your nervous system. Mistakes lose their emotional charge. They become procedural rather than personal.

Another aspect of repair is recognizing when the listener is already helping you. Many learners miss subtle cues: a rephrasing, a suggested word, a confirming nod. These are collaborative repairs initiated by the listener. When you accept them smoothly and continue, you reinforce cooperation. When you resist them out of pride or confusion, you create tension.

Repair strategies also apply to misunderstandings. Sometimes you realize mid-conversation that you have been interpreting something incorrectly. Admitting this briefly and adjusting course is far more effective than pretending everything is fine. Clarifying early prevents larger breakdowns later. Again, the emphasis is on brevity and forward motion.

Ultimately, repair is about trust. Trust that communication is resilient. Trust that listeners are not tallying your errors. Trust that you can recover and continue. When you internalize this trust, conversation stops feeling fragile. You can take risks, knowing you have tools to handle the consequences.

6.3 Asking Better Questions

Questions are one of the most powerful tools for conversation control. They shift the focus away from you, reduce pressure, and generate language you can respond to. Many learners underuse them or rely on rigid, memorized forms. Asking better questions transforms conversations from interrogations into exchanges.

A single well-placed question can open multiple paths. This is the idea behind question ladders. You start with a simple question, then build naturally based on the response. Each answer suggests a follow-up. You are not planning five questions in advance. You are listening and stepping forward one rung at a time.

This approach does two important things. It keeps you engaged, and it gives you thinking time. While the other person speaks, you process, select, and prepare your next move. The conversation becomes a rhythm of listening and responding, rather than a test of production speed.

Question ladders also reduce the need for complex language. You can ask meaningful questions with simple structures. What matters is relevance, not sophistication. When your questions connect to what the other person just said, they feel natural. You are not changing subjects abruptly; you are deepening the current one.

Open-ended prompts are especially useful because they encourage longer responses. Longer responses mean more input for you and less pressure to speak continuously. They also reveal vocabulary and structures you can reuse. This creates a virtuous cycle. The more the other person talks, the easier it becomes for you to stay engaged.

Asking open-ended questions does not mean being vague. Specific prompts that invite elaboration work best. They signal genuine interest. People enjoy talking about their experiences, opinions, and plans. When you tap into that, conversation flows more easily.

There is also a strategic advantage here. When the other person speaks more, you can focus on comprehension rather than production. This builds listening skills and reinforces patterns. You absorb language in context, which improves your own output later.

The topic steering wheel is the final piece of conversation control. Conversations naturally drift. Sometimes they stall. Being able to shift subjects smoothly keeps things alive. Abrupt changes feel awkward because they break continuity. Smooth transitions acknowledge what came before while introducing something new.

Steering does not require elaborate phrases. It requires sensitivity. You link the new topic to something already mentioned. This creates coherence. The listener feels guided rather than redirected. This skill is subtle but powerful. It allows you to avoid dead ends without drawing attention to the shift.

Good steering also respects energy. Some topics exhaust quickly. Others invite expansion. When you notice engagement dropping, you adjust. This is not manipulation; it is responsiveness. Conversation is a shared space. Steering helps maintain balance.

Asking better questions also changes how you see yourself in conversation. You are no longer someone struggling to express complex ideas. You are someone facilitating interaction. This role carries confidence. It reframes your purpose. You are not there to perform. You are there to connect.

Over time, these strategies compound. Repair becomes automatic. Questions become intuitive. You stop measuring success by how perfectly you spoke and start measuring it by how well the conversation flowed. This shift is profound. It aligns with how fluent speakers actually operate.

Conversation control is not about dominance or verbosity. It is about continuity, responsiveness, and adaptability. When you know how to repair, ask, and steer, you are never truly stuck. Even with limited language, you can keep the exchange alive. And keeping it alive is the essence of fluency.

Chapter 7 — Listening That Actually Works in Real Spanish

7.1 Decode the Speed Illusion

The first thing most learners say when they hear real Spanish is not "I don't know these words," but "they're speaking too fast." This reaction feels obvious and self-explanatory, yet it hides a misconception that slows progress for years. Native speakers are not speaking faster than your brain can handle. What feels like speed is actually compression. Spanish does not arrive one word at a time. It arrives in chunks, and until your ear learns to recognize those chunks, everything blends together.

The sensation of speed is created when your brain tries to do the wrong job. Beginners and intermediate learners often listen as if they were reading subtitles in their head. They expect to identify each word, map it to meaning, and then assemble the sentence. This approach works at very slow speeds and fails completely at natural ones. By the time you recognize the third word, the sentence has already moved on. The result is overload, not because the speech is fast, but because the strategy is inefficient.

Retraining your ear begins with accepting that you will not catch every word, and that you do not need to. Native listeners do not hear everything either. They predict. They infer. They rely on patterns and expectations. Their brains are not working harder; they are working differently. Listening is not passive reception. It is active interpretation.

The illusion of speed also comes from rhythm. As discussed earlier, Spanish has smooth syllable timing. Words flow into each other with fewer sharp pauses than in English. If you are listening for pauses between words, you will miss them. Spanish signals boundaries through melody and stress, not silence. Once you learn to listen for these cues, the stream begins to separate naturally.

Another factor is redundancy. Spanish repeats information across grammar, context, and vocabulary. When you catch part of the message, the rest often becomes predictable. Learners who focus too narrowly on individual words miss this redundancy. They assume that missing one word means missing everything. In reality, meaning often survives even when several words are unclear.

Chunk listening is the skill that resolves this problem. Instead of listening for words, you listen for units of meaning. These units can be phrases, common combinations, or familiar sentence frames. They arrive as wholes. When you recognize a chunk, you grasp meaning instantly, without translation. This is how native comprehension works.

At first, chunk listening feels imprecise. You may understand the general idea without being able to repeat the exact wording. This can feel unsatisfying if you equate understanding with precision. But in real life, understanding is functional. You know what is happening, what is being asked, and how to respond. That is success.

Training chunk listening involves shifting attention. Instead of straining to decode every sound, you relax your focus slightly and listen for shape. You notice how long a phrase lasts, where the speaker's voice rises or falls, and which parts sound familiar. Over time, these shapes become associated with meanings. Your ear builds a library of patterns.

This is also where prior chapters come together. The sentence structures you practiced earlier become anchors. When you hear the beginning of a familiar structure, your brain anticipates what may come next. This anticipation reduces cognitive load. You are no longer processing everything from scratch. You are matching what you hear to what you already know.

The "keyword capture" method accelerates this process. Instead of trying to understand everything, you deliberately listen for a small number of high-value words in each sentence. These are usually verbs, nouns, or time markers. Capturing even one or two of these can be enough to reconstruct meaning.

Keyword capture works because language is not evenly weighted. Some words carry more information than others. Articles, prepositions, and fillers often contribute less to core meaning. Verbs and key nouns carry the story. When you train yourself to identify these anchors, comprehension improves rapidly.

This method also reduces anxiety. You are no longer failing because you missed something. You are succeeding because you caught what matters. Each captured keyword reinforces confidence. Confidence keeps your attention open. Closed, anxious attention misses even more.

Another important aspect of decoding the speed illusion is exposure. Not passive exposure, but purposeful exposure. Listening improves when you know what you are listening for. If you listen aimlessly, your brain does not know which patterns to prioritize. When you listen with a strategy—chunk recognition or keyword capture—you give your brain a task it can learn from.

Repetition also plays a role, but not repetition of the same audio endlessly. Repetition of similar structures across different contexts is more effective. This teaches flexibility. You recognize the same chunk with slight variations. This recognition builds robustness. The pattern becomes stable even when the details change.

It is also crucial to manage expectations. Understanding real Spanish does not mean understanding everything. Even native speakers miss words, especially in noisy environments or emotional conversations. They rely on context and repair. Your goal is not total capture. It is sufficient understanding to participate.

As your ear retrains, something subtle happens. What once felt fast begins to feel normal. You still miss things, but you are not overwhelmed by it. You can stay present in the conversation. You can respond appropriately even when parts are unclear. This is functional listening.

The speed illusion dissolves when you stop chasing individual words and start trusting patterns. Spanish becomes less like a blur and more like a current you can ride. You are no longer fighting the flow. You are moving with it.

Decoding speed is therefore not about slowing Spanish down. It is about speeding your perception up by aligning it with how the language actually works. When you listen in chunks and capture keywords, real Spanish stops sounding impossibly fast and starts sounding richly layered. You may not hear every detail, but you hear enough. And in real conversation, enough is exactly what you need.

7.2 Accents, Slang, and Real-World Noise

The moment you step outside controlled learning environments, listening changes character. The Spanish you encounter is no longer neutral, careful, or designed for learners. It comes wrapped in accents, colored by slang, and layered with noise. Many learners interpret this shift as a sudden drop in ability. In reality, it is a change in conditions, not a loss of skill. The problem is not that you forgot Spanish; it is that your listening system has not yet been trained for variability.

Accent tolerance is the ability to stay calm and oriented when the sound of Spanish changes. Panic is the true enemy here. When you hear a new voice with unfamiliar pronunciation, your brain often reacts as if the language itself has changed. Attention narrows. You start listening harder, which paradoxically makes comprehension worse. Tolerance begins with accepting that Spanish has many legitimate sound shapes. None of them are "wrong." They are simply different distributions of the same underlying system.

Training accent tolerance is less about learning specific accents and more about learning how to respond to novelty. The first step is to stop expecting immediate understanding. When you hear a new accent, give yourself permission to understand less at first. This reduces pressure and keeps your listening flexible. As you relax, patterns emerge. The accent stops sounding chaotic and starts revealing its logic.

Most accents do not change everything. They emphasize different sounds, compress certain syllables, or stretch others. The core structures remain. When you listen for chunks and keywords, as discussed earlier, accents become variations rather than obstacles. You recognize the structure even when the surface changes.

Slang adds another layer of complexity. It can feel overwhelming because it seems infinite and constantly evolving. The mistake many learners make is trying to learn slang comprehensively. This is neither possible nor necessary. Slang triage is the skill of deciding what deserves attention and what can be safely ignored.

Some slang is high-frequency and widely understood. Other expressions are hyper-local or momentary. Your goal is not to speak slang fluently, but to recognize enough of it to avoid confusion. Recognition requires less effort than production. You do not need to use every term you hear. You need to know whether it matters for understanding.

Context helps enormously here. Slang often appears in predictable emotional zones: humor, frustration, enthusiasm, emphasis. Even when you do not know the exact meaning, you can often infer the function. Is the speaker joking? Complaining? Intensifying a point? Understanding function keeps you oriented even when vocabulary is missing.

Real-world noise is the final stress test. Cafés, streets, and group conversations introduce acoustic challenges that no app can fully simulate. Background sounds compete for attention. Multiple voices overlap. Speakers interrupt each other. These conditions strain working memory. The solution is not to strain harder, but to adjust strategy.

In noisy environments, selective listening becomes crucial. You cannot process everything. You choose what to prioritize. Often this means focusing on the main speaker or the main thread of conversation and letting peripheral details go. This is what native listeners do instinctively. They tune in and out dynamically.

Group conversations are particularly challenging because turn-taking is less predictable. Speakers jump in. Topics shift rapidly. Many learners feel lost because they try to track every contribution. A more sustainable approach is to anchor yourself to the general topic and listen for entry points. You do not need to understand every comment to participate meaningfully.

Listening in imperfect conditions is a skill that improves through exposure, but only if exposure is approached with the right mindset. If you enter these environments expecting failure, your brain closes down. If you enter expecting partial understanding and adaptation, your system stays flexible. Each experience adds to your tolerance. Over time, what once felt overwhelming becomes manageable.

7.3 Training Materials That Don't Bore You

Listening improves fastest when it is frequent and engaging. Boredom is not a minor inconvenience; it is a barrier to learning. When attention drops, the brain stops encoding. This is why many learners abandon listening practice despite knowing its importance. The solution is not more discipline, but better design.

Short clips are one of the most effective tools when used strategically. Long audio can be useful later, but early and intermediate stages benefit from concentrated exposure. A short clip allows repeated listening without fatigue. It also encourages active engagement. You can replay, pause, and focus on specific elements without losing the thread.

Replay rules matter. Listening repeatedly without a clear goal quickly becomes passive. Each replay should have a different focus. First, you listen for general meaning. Next, you listen for keywords. Then, you listen for rhythm or familiar chunks. This layered approach trains multiple skills at once and keeps the experience fresh.

Speed rules also play a role. Slowing audio slightly can be helpful initially, but relying on slow speed for too long creates dependency. The goal is to move toward natural speed as soon as possible. Alternating between slightly reduced speed and normal speed can help bridge the gap. Your ear learns that understanding at speed is possible.

Turning any audio into a practice system requires intention. A podcast, a video, or even a voice message can become training material if you interact with it actively. Passive listening has limited value. Active listening involves prediction, recall, and response. You ask yourself questions before and after listening. What do I expect to hear? What did I catch? What was unclear?

Your listening loop is the structure that keeps this practice sustainable. Daily exposure builds familiarity. Weekly variation builds flexibility. Periodic checkpoints measure progress. The exact format matters less than consistency. A loop ensures that listening is not an occasional activity, but an integrated part of your routine.

Daily listening does not need to be long. Even a few focused minutes can be effective if they are deliberate. Weekly sessions can be longer and more exploratory. Checkpoints provide motivation. When you revisit material that once felt incomprehensible and find it easier, progress becomes tangible.

Variety within the loop prevents stagnation. Different voices, topics, and contexts expand your tolerance. At the same time, some repetition is necessary for consolidation. Balancing novelty and familiarity keeps your brain challenged but not overwhelmed.

Training materials should also reflect your interests. When content aligns with what you care about, motivation rises naturally. You listen not because you should, but because you want to. This intrinsic motivation sustains long-term practice better than any external plan.

Ultimately, listening is not a passive skill you acquire by osmosis. It is an active process of pattern recognition and adaptation. When you choose materials thoughtfully and interact with them intentionally, listening stops feeling like a chore. It becomes exploration.

As your system develops, you notice a shift. Accents become interesting rather than threatening. Slang becomes texture rather than noise. Imperfect conditions become manageable rather than paralyzing. This shift marks real listening competence.

By training your ear to handle variability and designing practice that engages you, you build a listening ability that works in the real world. Spanish stops sounding like a test and starts sounding like communication. And communication, even when imperfect, is where understanding truly lives.

Chapter 8 — Speaking Like a Human: Naturalness, Politeness, and Style

8.1 Politeness and Tone (Without Sounding Stiff)

Reaching the point where people understand you is a milestone. Reaching the point where people feel comfortable with you is something else entirely. Naturalness in Spanish is not primarily about advanced vocabulary or flawless grammar. It is about tone. Tone shapes how your words land. The same sentence can feel friendly, abrupt, or even rude depending on how it is delivered. This is why politeness is not an optional add-on. It is a core speaking skill.

Many learners approach politeness with caution. They fear sounding stiff, formal, or artificial. This fear is justified, because politeness is often taught through rigid formulas that do not reflect real speech. In everyday Spanish, politeness is usually light, subtle, and woven into rhythm rather than spelled out. Understanding this frees you from the false choice between sounding rude and sounding robotic.

Polite shortcuts are the foundation of natural tone. These are small linguistic adjustments that soften speech without adding length or complexity. They do not announce politeness; they imply it. When used well, they become almost invisible. This invisibility is their strength. You sound respectful without sounding rehearsed.

One of the most important shifts is understanding that politeness in Spanish often lives in the verb rather than in extra words. Slight changes in how you frame a request or suggestion can transform its impact. Instead of issuing direct commands, speakers often lean toward phrasing that sounds cooperative. This does not weaken your message. It aligns it with social expectations.

Directness is not inherently rude. Spanish can be very direct. The problem arises when directness is stripped of warmth. Warmth is conveyed through tone, pacing, and small softeners that signal goodwill. When these elements are missing, even neutral statements can sound harsh to a Spanish ear.

Softening direct speech does not require avoiding clarity. It requires adding a human layer. This might mean framing a statement as a preference rather than a demand, or acknowledging the other person's perspective briefly before stating your own. These adjustments are not about submission. They are about mutual respect.

Many learners overcompensate by apologizing excessively. They apologize for their Spanish, for asking questions, for existing in the conversation. While this may feel polite, it often has the opposite effect. It places emotional labor on the listener and frames the interaction as a burden. Friendly confidence is more appealing than constant self-effacement.

Friendly confidence comes from assuming goodwill. You speak as if you are welcome, not as if you are intruding. This does not mean ignoring mistakes or acting entitled. It means trusting that communication is a shared goal. When you adopt this stance, your tone shifts naturally. You sound more relaxed. People respond in kind.

Politeness also varies by context, but certain shortcuts work almost everywhere. These are not formal titles or honorifics, but conversational habits. Brief acknowledgments, expressions of appreciation, and small gestures of consideration go a long way. They do not slow conversation. They smooth it.

Another common trap is translating politeness directly from your native language. What sounds polite in one language can sound distant or exaggerated in another. Spanish often prefers warmth over distance. Overly formal phrasing can create separation rather than respect. Learning to sound natural means letting go of literal translation and tuning into local norms.

Tone is also influenced by rhythm and intonation. A sentence delivered with rising intonation can sound tentative or inviting. The same sentence delivered flatly can sound cold. You do not need to master musical nuance, but you do need to be aware that tone carries meaning beyond words. Listening closely to how people soften requests and respond to each other provides models you can adapt.

Politeness without stiffness also involves knowing when not to soften. Over-softening can dilute your message and make you sound unsure. Natural speech balances clarity and courtesy. You state what you need, but you do so with consideration. This balance is dynamic. It adjusts based on relationship, setting, and purpose.

As you develop this sensitivity, you may notice that people react differently to you even if your grammar has not changed. Conversations feel easier. Requests are met with cooperation. Small talk flows more smoothly. These changes are not accidental. They reflect your growing control over tone.

Speaking like a human means embracing imperfection while prioritizing connection. You do not need to get everything right. You need to show that you are present, respectful, and engaged. Politeness supports this presence. It signals that you care about how your words affect others.

This chapter is not about memorizing polite phrases. It is about understanding the social logic behind them. Once you understand that logic, you can generate your own polite language naturally. You are no longer choosing between being understood and being liked. You are doing both.

Naturalness emerges when politeness becomes intuitive rather than calculated. You stop thinking, "How do I sound?" and start noticing, "How does this land?" That shift marks a deeper level of fluency. You are no longer just speaking Spanish. You are participating in Spanish interactions as yourself.

Being understood opens the door. Sounding natural invites people in. And it is through these softer skills—tone, warmth, and restraint—that Spanish stops feeling like a performance and starts feeling like a relationship.

8.2 The Spanish "Feel": Filler Words, Reactions, and Flow

At some point in learning Spanish, you reach a strange threshold. People understand you. You can get things done. You can explain, ask, and respond. Yet something still feels off. Conversations move, but they do not quite flow. This gap is not about grammar or vocabulary. It is about feel. Languages carry a social rhythm, a set of small signals that show you are present, responsive, and emotionally aligned. In Spanish, much of this feel lives in filler words, reactions, and the subtle mechanics of flow.

Filler words are often misunderstood. Learners think of them as empty sounds, things to avoid. In reality, they are structural. They hold conversational space. They signal attention, agreement, surprise, or hesitation. When used naturally, they make speech feel alive. When absent, even correct sentences can sound abrupt or distant.

Natural reactions are the fastest way to sound more human in Spanish. Short responses like expressions of agreement or acknowledgment do not add information, but they add connection. They show that you are listening, not just waiting to speak. In many Spanish-speaking contexts, silence where a reaction is expected can feel uncomfortable or even dismissive. A brief verbal signal reassures the speaker that you are with them.

Timing matters more than variety here. You do not need a large inventory of reactions. A small set used appropriately is enough. The key is to let reactions arise naturally from the conversation rather than inserting them mechanically. When something is clear, you acknowledge it. When something is positive, you respond. These moments are not interruptions. They are part of the rhythm.

Conversational glue goes beyond reactions. It includes small connectors and phrases that link ideas smoothly. These elements prevent your speech from sounding like a series of isolated statements. They create continuity. With them, sentences lean into each other. Without them, speech feels segmented.

This glue often appears in transitions. You finish one idea and move to the next. You agree and then add a detail. You acknowledge and then redirect. These moves happen constantly in natural conversation. When learners lack the tools to make them, they either stop abruptly or over-explain. Both disrupt flow.

The challenge is balance. Overusing fillers or reactions can sound exaggerated or repetitive. Underusing them can make you sound stiff. Naturalness lives in moderation. You listen first, then respond in proportion to what you hear. This proportionality is learned through exposure and imitation, not rules.

Avoiding overuse requires awareness. Many learners latch onto one or two expressions they like and repeat them constantly. This happens because those expressions feel safe. Over time, they become noticeable. Native speakers vary reactions instinctively or sometimes choose silence. Silence, when intentional, is also part of flow. The goal is not to fill every gap, but to respond when response adds value.

Flow also depends on pacing. Spanish conversation often moves quickly, but not hurriedly. Speakers overlap slightly, react mid-sentence, and pick up threads without formal handoffs. When you allow yourself to react in real time rather than waiting for perfect pauses, you align with this rhythm. This does not mean interrupting aggressively. It means participating actively.

As you develop sensitivity to flow, you start feeling when a reaction fits and when it does not. This feeling cannot be memorized. It emerges from listening and experimenting. Occasionally you will misjudge. That is part of learning. What matters is staying engaged rather than retreating into silence.

8.3 Cultural Conversation Patterns

Language does not exist in a vacuum. It lives inside cultural patterns of interaction. Understanding these patterns helps you interpret what is happening and choose how to respond. Without this understanding, even fluent language can feel awkward. You may know what to say but not when or how to say it.

Turn-taking is a key example. In many Spanish-speaking contexts, conversation is more overlapping than in some other cultures. People jump in to show enthusiasm or agreement, not to dominate. For learners, this can feel chaotic or rude. In reality, it is often a sign of engagement. Silence is not always respectful. Sometimes it signals disinterest.

Learning how interruptions work requires reframing. Not every interruption is a challenge. Many are collaborative. A brief interjection can show that you are following closely. The art lies in reading the energy of the exchange. When the tone is animated and friendly, overlap is normal. When the tone is serious or formal, more spacing is expected.

Small talk also functions differently than many learners expect. It is not an empty ritual. It is a bridge. Conversations often begin with safe, shared topics before moving into more personal or substantive areas. Weather, daily routines, and immediate surroundings are not endpoints. They are launchpads.

Knowing how to transition is crucial. You acknowledge the small talk and then connect it to something else. This connection can be simple. You relate the topic to a shared experience or a question. These transitions keep conversation from stalling without forcing depth prematurely.

Humor and warmth play a central role in Spanish interaction. Humor does not require advanced vocabulary. Often it is situational, observational, or self-referential. A light comment, a playful exaggeration, or a shared laugh builds rapport. Warmth is conveyed through tone and openness more than through clever wording.

Many learners avoid humor out of fear of misunderstanding or being inappropriate. This caution is understandable, but total avoidance can make interactions feel flat. You do not need to be funny. You need to be responsive. Smiling, reacting positively, and showing curiosity are forms of warmth that do not risk offense.

Cultural patterns also influence how opinions are expressed. Disagreement is often softened or framed relationally. Direct confrontation is not always the default. Understanding this helps you interpret responses correctly. What sounds vague may be polite. What sounds indirect may be considerate.

As you internalize these patterns, conversations begin to feel less scripted. You stop worrying about taking the "right" turn and start responding to what is happening. This responsiveness is the core of naturalness. You are no longer translating culture in your head. You are participating in it.

Speaking like a human in Spanish is not about copying natives perfectly. It is about aligning with the social logic of the language. Filler words, reactions, and flow are tools for that alignment. Cultural patterns provide the context that gives those tools meaning.

When you combine these elements, something shifts. Conversations feel less effortful. You are not constantly monitoring yourself. You are listening, reacting, and adjusting. Mistakes still happen, but they matter less because connection is intact.

This is the final layer of fluency. Not the ability to say everything, but the ability to belong in the conversation. And that belonging comes from mastering the soft skills that make language feel alive.

Chapter 9 — The 60-Day System: Your Daily Routine and Weekly Checkpoints

9.1 The Daily Flow Routine (20–40 Minutes)

Most language plans fail not because they are poorly designed, but because they are unsustainable. They demand motivation on days when motivation is unavailable. They assume ideal conditions. They rely on intensity instead of rhythm. The 60-day system works because it accepts a simple truth: consistency beats intensity. Twenty minutes, done almost every day, reshapes habits in a way that sporadic effort never can. This routine is not built to impress. It is built to survive real life.

The daily flow routine is deliberately modest. It fits into mornings, lunch breaks, evenings, or transitional moments. It can expand when you have time and contract when you do not. What matters is not exact duration, but continuity. Each session reinforces the previous one, creating a chain your brain learns to expect. Over sixty days, this expectation becomes automatic. Spanish stops being something you "try to fit in" and becomes something that happens.

The routine unfolds in three phases that mirror how skill acquisition actually works. You prepare the system, you challenge it, and then you express. Skipping any of these weakens the effect. Together, they create momentum without exhaustion.

The warm-up exists to shift your brain into Spanish mode. Five minutes is enough. You are not learning new material here. You are waking up patterns that already exist. Pronunciation is especially effective at this stage because it engages the body.

Your mouth, breath, and rhythm align with the language before your mind starts analyzing. This physical alignment reduces friction later.

Quick recall is the second part of the warm-up. You reach for words and structures you already know and bring them to the surface. This is not review in the traditional sense. You are not checking lists. You are activating access. When recall is fast and light, speaking feels less effortful. The goal is not correctness, but readiness.

This warm-up phase also serves a psychological function. It lowers the activation energy of the session. Starting is often the hardest part. Five minutes feels manageable even on difficult days. Once you start, continuing becomes easier. This is not accidental. The routine is designed to remove excuses.

The core phase is where growth happens. This is where you stretch your ability slightly beyond comfort. Ten to twenty minutes is the sweet spot. Less than that, and the challenge is insufficient. More than that, and fatigue undermines quality. In this phase, you work with speaking prompts and sentence-building, not passive input.

Speaking prompts are effective because they create purpose. You are not speaking randomly. You are responding to a situation, a question, or a constraint. This mirrors real conversation. The prompt gives your brain a problem to solve. Solving problems is how skills are built.

Sentence-building at this stage focuses on recombination. You reuse familiar structures with new content. This reinforces flexibility. You are not memorizing new sentences. You are practicing assembling meaning under light pressure. This assembly process is where fluency emerges.

Importantly, the core phase should feel slightly uncomfortable but not overwhelming. If you feel lost, the prompt is too complex. If you feel bored, it is too easy. Adjusting difficulty is part of the system. You are not following a rigid syllabus. You are responding to your current state.

The final phase is output. This is where many learners hesitate, yet it is the most transformative part of the routine. Output turns internal practice into external behavior. Recording yourself, shadowing audio, or engaging in a short conversation forces integration. It reveals gaps you cannot see while thinking silently.

Recording is powerful because it creates distance. You hear yourself as a listener would. This perspective highlights rhythm, clarity, and flow more effectively than mental monitoring. It also builds resilience. Hearing your own imperfect Spanish regularly reduces self-consciousness. The voice becomes familiar. Fear diminishes.

Shadowing, when done briefly, reinforces timing and intonation. It aligns your speech with natural rhythm without requiring invention. This is particularly useful on low-energy days. You still produce sound. You still train the system. Momentum is preserved.

Short conversations, even with yourself or a partner, complete the cycle. They remind you why you are practicing. Language exists to connect. Even a few minutes of real interaction anchor the routine in reality. They also provide emotional feedback. A successful exchange, however small, reinforces commitment.

The output phase can range from five to fifteen minutes depending on time and energy. On busy days, five minutes is enough. On open days, you can extend. The system accommodates both. What matters is that output happens regularly. Without it, progress remains theoretical.

One of the strengths of this routine is that it creates a feedback loop. Warm-up prepares access. Core challenges build capacity. Output tests integration. The results of output inform the next warm-up. You notice what felt weak or strong and adjust. Learning becomes responsive rather than linear.

This routine also respects cognitive limits. It alternates focus. You are not grinding the same skill for forty minutes. You are moving through different modes of engagement. This variety keeps attention alive and reduces burnout.

Over time, the routine builds trust. You trust that showing up for twenty minutes is enough. You stop worrying about missing days occasionally because the system is resilient. One missed day does not break the chain. You return the next day without guilt. Guilt is replaced by continuity.

Another important effect is identity shift. When you practice daily, even briefly, you stop seeing yourself as someone who is "trying to learn Spanish" and start seeing yourself as someone who uses Spanish regularly. This identity change influences behavior outside the routine. You notice opportunities to listen, speak, or think in Spanish during the day. The language leaks into life.

The daily flow routine is not about optimization. It is about alignment. It aligns with how habits form, how skills develop, and how adults actually live. It does not demand perfection. It rewards persistence.

At the end of sixty days, the transformation is not dramatic in any single session. It is cumulative. You speak with less hesitation. You recover faster. You understand more than you expect. These gains feel natural because they were built gradually.

This is the power of consistency. Not heroic effort, but repeated presence. The daily flow routine gives you a structure that carries you when motivation fades and accelerates you when motivation appears. It is not a challenge to conquer. It is a rhythm to inhabit. And once that rhythm is established, Spanish stops being something you chase and becomes something you practice—daily, calmly, and with growing confidence.

9.2 Weekly Checkpoints That Guarantee Progress

Daily practice builds momentum, but weekly checkpoints give that momentum direction. Without checkpoints, effort can blur into routine. You show up, you do the work, yet you are not always sure what is changing. Checkpoints exist to answer a simple question: is this working? They prevent drift, reinforce confidence, and provide clear signals about what to adjust next.

Weekly goals are not about covering material. They are about shifting capability. Each week emphasizes a different dimension of speaking so that progress is balanced rather than lopsided. Early gains often appear in clarity. Your pronunciation stabilizes, your rhythm smooths out, and people ask you to repeat less. This is not accidental. It reflects focused attention on being understandable rather than impressive.

As clarity improves, speed becomes the next natural focus. Speed does not mean talking fast. It means responding without long pauses. At the weekly level, speed is measured by reduced hesitation, not increased output. You notice that answers come quicker, even if they are still simple. This is a significant milestone. It means access is improving.

Vocabulary growth follows, but not in isolation. You are not counting words. You are noticing how often you reach for a word and find it available. This availability matters more than breadth. Weekly reflection helps you see which words are sticking and which ones are not yet integrated. It guides your selection for the next week.

Control emerges as you combine clarity, speed, and vocabulary. You begin steering conversations rather than reacting. You ask questions, shift topics, and recover from gaps smoothly. Control is subtle. It shows up as ease. Conversations feel less fragile. You are not afraid of mistakes because you know how to handle them.

Confidence is the cumulative effect of these shifts. It is not a feeling you chase. It is a behavior you notice. You speak more willingly. You volunteer comments. You stay in Spanish longer before switching. Weekly checkpoints help you recognize these changes, which might otherwise go unnoticed.

Mini-tests make these observations concrete. They are not exams. They are snapshots. You speak for a set amount of time on a familiar topic without stopping. You listen to a short clip and summarize the main idea. You record yourself and notice patterns. These tests can be done alone and take only a few minutes, but they provide powerful feedback.

Speaking benchmarks reveal whether your language holds together under light pressure. You are not aiming for eloquence. You are aiming for continuity. Can you keep talking? Can you recover when you get stuck? These questions matter more than correctness.

Listening benchmarks show whether your ear is adapting. You may not understand everything, but you should grasp more than before. Noticing improvement in listening often lags behind speaking, so weekly checks prevent discouragement. You see progress that daily practice may obscure.

Adjusting the plan when you miss days is a critical skill. Life happens. Travel, illness, work, and fatigue disrupt routines. The danger is not missing days; it is interpreting missed days as failure. When that happens, many learners abandon the system entirely.

The 60-day system is designed to absorb disruption. If you miss days, you do not "catch up" by doubling effort. You return to the routine at the next opportunity. Weekly checkpoints help you recalibrate without judgment. You assess honestly and adjust volume or focus slightly if needed.

This flexibility preserves momentum. You stay engaged because the system feels humane. Progress continues because consistency is measured over weeks, not days. This perspective shift is essential for long-term success.

9.3 Building a Practice Ecosystem

No routine survives in isolation. To sustain practice over sixty days, you need an environment that supports it. This environment is not physical space alone. It is a network of cues, relationships, and structures that make practice feel natural rather than forced.

Finding conversation partners is often a source of anxiety. Many learners worry about awkwardness or imposition. The key is reframing. Conversation is not a favor you ask; it is an exchange. You bring curiosity, attention, and effort. Those are valuable. When you approach interactions with this mindset, the dynamic changes.

Starting small helps. Short, low-pressure interactions build familiarity. Over time, these interactions feel less formal and more conversational. You are no longer "practicing Spanish." You are talking to someone. This shift reduces self-consciousness and increases frequency.

Accountability reinforces consistency. When practice is private, it is easy to postpone. When it is visible, even minimally, commitment strengthens. Accountability does not require external pressure. Simple logs, personal challenges, or sharing goals with others can be enough. The point is not surveillance. It is awareness.

Tracking practice creates a feedback loop. You see patterns. You notice which days are harder and which are easier. This information allows you to adjust proactively. Logs also provide evidence of effort. On days when motivation dips, seeing a record of consistency helps you continue.

Public commitments add another layer. Declaring an intention, even casually, increases follow-through. This does not mean announcing ambitious goals. It means stating what you are doing now. The present focus keeps pressure low and relevance high.

Reducing friction is perhaps the most important aspect of building an ecosystem. Practice should be easy to start. Materials should be accessible. Decisions should be minimized. When starting requires too many steps, resistance grows.

Small design choices matter. Keeping resources in one place. Scheduling practice at a consistent time. Preparing prompts in advance. These adjustments remove obstacles before they appear. When the barrier to entry is low, consistency increases naturally.

An effective ecosystem also includes recovery strategies. On low-energy days, you do not skip entirely. You downshift. You do the minimum version of the routine. This preserves the habit loop. Tomorrow becomes easier because today was not abandoned.

Over sixty days, this ecosystem compounds. Practice feels less like effort and more like routine. Spanish becomes part of your day, not an extra task. This integration is the real achievement.

The 60-day system works because it aligns effort with structure. Daily routines create momentum. Weekly checkpoints provide direction. An ecosystem sustains both. Together, they transform practice from a struggle into a habit.

At the end of the process, progress feels earned but not exhausting. You have not burned out. You have not relied on bursts of motivation. You have built a system that carries you forward. And that system, once established, does not end at sixty days. It becomes a foundation you can return to, adapt, and extend as your Spanish continues to grow.

Chapter 10 — Real-Life Scenarios: Travel, Work, Dating, Friends, and Everything Between

10.1 Travel and Everyday Life

Fluency becomes real the moment language leaves the page and enters a situation. Until then, it is potential. Travel and everyday life are where that potential is tested—not in dramatic conversations, but in ordinary moments where things must be done, decisions made, and problems resolved. This is where confidence either solidifies or evaporates. The good news is that most daily situations run on predictable patterns. When you master those patterns, your confidence does not depend on inspiration. It depends on recognition.

Ordering food, asking for directions, checking in, paying, clarifying a mistake, explaining a problem—these moments repeat everywhere. They are emotionally loaded because they involve time pressure, social exposure, and practical consequences. Yet linguistically, they are simple. What overwhelms learners is not complexity, but stakes. You are hungry. You are tired. There is a line behind you. The words you know suddenly feel far away.

Essential scripts exist to handle these situations smoothly. A script is not something you recite robotically. It is a reliable starting point that gives you footing. Once you are standing, you can adjust. The purpose of a script is not to say everything perfectly, but to prevent freezing. When you know how to begin, the rest follows more easily.

Ordering, for example, is less about food vocabulary than about structure. You are making a request, confirming details, and closing the exchange. The same structure applies whether you are ordering coffee, buying a ticket, or requesting a service. When you internalize the structure, you stop worrying about every word. You focus on the interaction.

Directions work similarly. You do not need to understand every detail to succeed. You need to identify landmarks, confirm orientation, and check understanding. Many learners expect to follow directions perfectly the first time. Native speakers do not. They ask again. They clarify. They adjust. Treating this as normal removes pressure.

Checking in at a hotel or apartment often triggers anxiety because it feels formal. In reality, it is highly scripted. Identification, confirmation, timing, and questions follow a predictable sequence. When you recognize this sequence, you stop improvising unnecessarily. You listen for cues and respond within the expected frame.

Problem-solving is where confidence is truly tested. Something is wrong. A reservation is missing. An order is incorrect. A service did not work. In these moments, learners often switch to English out of fear of escalation. This is understandable, but it robs you of growth. Handling small problems calmly in Spanish builds disproportionate confidence.

The key to problem-solving is tone, not vocabulary. You do not need elaborate language. You need respectful confidence. Respectful confidence means you are polite without being apologetic, clear without being aggressive. You state the issue as a shared problem, not a personal complaint. This framing invites cooperation.

Phrases that open doors often do so because they reduce social friction. They acknowledge effort, show patience, and signal reasonableness. When you approach interactions with this attitude, people respond generously. Language becomes a bridge rather than a barrier.

Handling misunderstandings calmly is a skill that applies everywhere. Misunderstandings are inevitable. The difference between a stressful experience and a manageable one lies in response. When you treat misunderstanding as a normal part of communication, you stay present. You rephrase. You confirm. You slow down. You do not interpret confusion as failure.

Switching to English often feels like relief, but it can undermine confidence long-term. Each time you stay in Spanish and resolve a misunderstanding, you reinforce self-trust. You prove to yourself that you can navigate uncertainty. This proof accumulates. Over time, the urge to switch diminishes because you no longer see Spanish as fragile.

Everyday life also includes small social exchanges that are easy to overlook. Greetings, brief comments, acknowledgments. These moments matter because they shape how you are perceived and how you feel. When you participate, even minimally, you signal belonging. Belonging reduces anxiety.

Respectful confidence shows up here as well. You greet people naturally. You respond when spoken to. You do not over-explain or withdraw. These behaviors communicate comfort more than perfect language ever could.

One of the most powerful shifts happens when you stop treating travel Spanish as a special category and start seeing it as everyday Spanish. Travel compresses life. You eat, move, interact, and solve problems in quick succession. This intensity accelerates learning if you stay engaged. Each interaction reinforces patterns. Each success builds momentum.

Confidence skyrockets not because you suddenly know more, but because you recognize situations. Recognition reduces cognitive load. You are not inventing language. You are applying known solutions to familiar problems. This is situational fluency.

Situational fluency also adapts easily. Once you master a few core scenarios, others feel approachable. A restaurant leads to a café. A hotel leads to an office. A shop leads to a pharmacy. Structures repeat. Only details change.

The goal of this chapter is not to cover every possible situation. It is to change how you approach them. You are not walking into the unknown. You are entering variations of situations you already understand. When you carry this mindset, fear diminishes.

Real-life Spanish rewards presence over precision. People care that you are trying, that you are respectful, that you are clear enough to work together. They do not expect perfection. They expect participation.

Travel and everyday life are not tests of fluency. They are training grounds. Each interaction is an opportunity to practice calm, clarity, and confidence. When you stop aiming to impress and start aiming to engage, Spanish becomes a tool you trust.

Master these situations, and your confidence does not depend on mood or memory. It rests on experience. You have been here before. You know how this goes. And that knowing—quiet, practical, earned—is what real fluency feels like.

10.2 Work and Professional Spanish

Professional settings expose a different layer of fluency pressure. At work, language is tied to competence, credibility, and trust. Many learners feel that their Spanish collapses the moment the conversation turns professional, not because they lack intelligence or experience, but because they believe professionalism requires complexity. In reality, professional Spanish favors clarity, structure, and restraint. You do not need elaborate grammar to sound competent. You need control.

Meetings, emails, and introductions operate on predictable templates. These templates exist to reduce ambiguity and keep interactions efficient. When you understand this, professional Spanish stops feeling like an advanced domain reserved for near-native speakers and starts feeling like a system you can step into.

Introductions are a good example. In professional contexts, introductions are not about self-expression; they are about positioning. You state who you are, what you do, and why you are relevant to the conversation. This can be done with simple present tense structures and a calm tone. Overloading introductions with detail often creates confusion rather than authority. Conciseness signals confidence.

Meetings follow similar logic. You are rarely required to produce long monologues. Most contributions involve agreeing, clarifying, asking for input, or summarizing. These functions rely on a small set of recurring patterns. When you master these patterns, participation becomes manageable. You stop waiting for the perfect moment and start engaging naturally.

Emails amplify this effect. Written Spanish in professional settings is often more formal than speech, but it is also highly conventional. Greetings, transitions, requests, and closings repeat across industries. You do not need to reinvent them. Using established phrasing signals competence because it aligns with expectations. Creativity is not the goal here. Reliability is.

Negotiation introduces emotional complexity. You may worry that your limited Spanish will make you sound weak or indecisive. This fear often leads learners to either over-soften their language or avoid negotiation entirely. Neither is necessary. Polite firmness is achievable with simple structures and clear intent.

Polite firmness means stating what you need or propose without aggression and without apology. You acknowledge the other side while maintaining your position. This balance does not require complex grammar. It requires controlled phrasing and steady tone. When you frame negotiation as problem-solving rather than confrontation, language becomes less intimidating.

Explaining your skills and background is another area where learners often overcomplicate. They try to compress years of experience into nuanced descriptions and get lost. A more effective approach is modular. You describe your role, your main responsibilities, and one or two concrete examples. This structure keeps explanations grounded.

Simplicity here is an asset. Clear descriptions build trust. You can always add detail if asked. When you speak plainly about what you do, listeners focus on content rather than form. This shifts attention away from your language level and onto your expertise.

Professional Spanish also benefits from controlled pacing. Speaking slightly slower than native speed is acceptable and often perceived as thoughtful. Rushing increases error and anxiety. Calm delivery reinforces authority. Authority in language is often about how you say things, not how many words you use.

As you gain experience, you begin to notice that professional interactions are forgiving. Colleagues care about outcomes. They adapt. They meet you halfway. When you show preparation and respect, language imperfections fade into the background.

The breakthrough comes when you stop seeing professional Spanish as a performance and start seeing it as collaboration. You are there to work together, not to impress linguistically. Once that mindset shifts, confidence follows.

10.3 Social Life and Connection

If professional Spanish tests competence, social Spanish tests belonging. Making friends, dating, and building connections expose different vulnerabilities. Here, the fear is not sounding unprofessional, but sounding awkward, distant, or misunderstood. Social fluency is less about precision and more about presence.

Making friends begins with invitations and follow-ups. These actions seem simple, yet they carry emotional weight. Inviting someone suggests openness. Following up suggests interest. Many learners hesitate here, worried about imposing or phrasing things incorrectly. This hesitation often leads to missed opportunities.

Social invitations in Spanish do not require elaborate phrasing. They require warmth and clarity. You suggest an activity, indicate timing loosely, and leave room for response. Over-planning can feel rigid. Under-planning can feel vague. Finding the middle ground comes with practice.

Follow-ups are equally important. They show reliability. A brief message confirming or adjusting plans maintains momentum.

When learners avoid follow-ups out of fear of bothering someone, connections fade. Understanding that follow-ups are normal, not intrusive, changes behavior.

Friendly small talk is the bridge that sustains these interactions. It is not about exchanging information; it is about signaling availability. Comments about shared experiences, immediate surroundings, or recent events create continuity. These topics are safe because they are mutual. They do not require deep disclosure.

Dating introduces additional sensitivity. Language choices here carry emotional and social implications. Respect, playfulness, and safety are paramount. Many learners fear flirting because they associate it with complex language or cultural nuance. In practice, dating communication often relies on tone more than vocabulary.

Playfulness can be conveyed through light comments, humor, and responsiveness. You do not need clever wordplay. You need attentiveness. Respect shows in pacing, listening, and consent. Clear communication is attractive. Ambiguity created by language limitations can be navigated through honesty.

Dating also tests emotional resilience. Misunderstandings happen. Signals are misread. Staying calm and open prevents escalation. Using Spanish imperfectly but sincerely often builds more connection than switching to English to appear smoother.

One of the biggest challenges in social settings is staying in Spanish longer. The English escape hatch appears when conversations deepen or when fatigue sets in. Switching feels easier. It restores fluency instantly. But it also halts growth.

Resisting this switch does not mean refusing English categorically. It means choosing Spanish when the conversation can support it. You can set expectations early by continuing in Spanish even when others switch. Often, people follow your lead.

Another strategy is to anchor the conversation in Spanish topics. When you discuss experiences, places, or routines connected to the Spanish-speaking context, the language feels appropriate. English feels less necessary.

Staying longer also requires tolerance for imperfection. Social conversations are unpredictable. You will miss jokes. You will search for words. Accepting this as part of connection reduces the urge to escape. You are not failing socially because your Spanish is imperfect. You are participating socially because you are present.

Over time, these choices compound. Friends get used to speaking Spanish with you. Dating feels less performative. You stop measuring each sentence. You start enjoying interaction.

Social fluency is not about mastering slang or humor. It is about reliability and warmth. People respond to how you make them feel. When you are attentive, respectful, and engaged, language becomes a secondary factor.

The real reward of situational fluency appears here. Spanish stops being something you use to survive situations and becomes something you use to connect. Work conversations feel collaborative. Social interactions feel natural. You are no longer switching identities when you switch languages.

Mastering work and social scenarios completes the arc of real-life fluency. You are not fluent in theory. You are fluent in practice. You can show up, contribute, and belong. And that belonging—earned through repeated, imperfect interaction—is what gives Spanish its deepest meaning.

Conclusion

Language is not a subject. It's a skill. That single distinction explains why so many intelligent, motivated people spend years "studying" Spanish and still freeze when someone asks them a simple question. Subjects reward memorization, endurance, and delayed performance. Skills reward action, feedback, and repetition under real conditions. You don't learn to swim by reading about water, and you don't learn to speak by waiting until you feel ready. You learn by entering the environment, making imperfect movements, and adjusting as you go. Language follows the same rules, even though most traditional methods pretend it doesn't.

Skills grow fastest when the feedback loop is short. You try, something happens, you notice, and you adapt. Long study sessions stretch that loop until it breaks. You consume information, feel productive, and postpone the moment of truth. Then, days or weeks later, you finally try to speak and discover that the knowledge didn't convert into action. This is not a personal flaw. It's a structural one. The system you used optimized for knowing about Spanish, not for using it.

The 60-day advantage exists because it aligns language learning with how skills actually form. Sixty days is long enough to rewire habits, but short enough to maintain urgency. Daily micro-habits keep the loop tight. Weekly checkpoints keep direction clear. Speaking from Day 1 prevents the most damaging illusion of all: the belief that fluency begins after preparation. In reality, fluency emerges during use.

This book is built around a specific outcome: Spanish Flow. Flow is not perfection. It is speed, clarity, and confidence moving together. Speed means you respond without translating every sentence in your head. Clarity means people understand you without strain, even if your grammar isn't flawless. Confidence means you stay in the conversation when things go wrong instead of retreating or switching languages. When these three align, Spanish stops feeling fragile. You are no longer protecting it. You are using it.

Most learners chase accuracy first and hope confidence will follow. It rarely does. Confidence is not the result of getting things right; it is the result of surviving getting things wrong. Flow emerges when you trust your ability to recover. That trust cannot be taught abstractly. It must be experienced repeatedly. This is why the structure of the next sixty days matters more than the amount of information you consume.

The system you are about to use is deliberately simple. Each day has a clear purpose and a manageable time window. The goal is not to impress yourself with effort, but to show up consistently. Daily practice keeps Spanish active in your nervous system. Weekly checkpoints prevent drift and give you evidence of progress. Talking from Day 1 ensures that every new word, sound, or structure attaches to real use instead of floating in isolation.

Before any of that works, however, you need to understand your personal baseline. Everyone brings a different history to Spanish. Some people tense up the moment they open their mouth. Others rush and lose coherence. Some apologize constantly. Others stay silent and hope the moment passes. These patterns are not random. They are stress responses. If you ignore them, they will quietly control your behavior no matter how much vocabulary you learn.

Stress triggers vary. For some, it's being corrected. For others, it's speaking in front of more than one person. For others, it's time pressure or unfamiliar accents. Confidence blockers hide behind reasonable-sounding thoughts: "I need to know more first," "I don't want to sound stupid," "I'll speak when I'm ready." These thoughts feel protective, but they delay the very exposure that would dissolve them. Naming them changes their power. Once you recognize your triggers, you can design practice that works with them instead of against them.

Equally important is defining your minimum viable Spanish. This is not an aspirational version of yourself giving a perfect presentation or debating abstract ideas. It is the smallest version of Spanish that would meaningfully improve your life right now. Ordering without anxiety. Holding a five-minute conversation. Explaining what you do. Navigating daily interactions without switching languages. When you define this minimum, practice gains direction. You stop measuring yourself against an imaginary finish line and start consolidating real capability.

Everything in this book is designed to build from that baseline outward. Chapter by chapter, you will install systems rather than collect tips. You will learn how to speak before you feel ready, how to handle anxiety when it appears, and how to adopt a Spanish identity that reduces self-consciousness instead of amplifying it. You will work on pronunciation not to sound impressive, but to be instantly understandable. You will train rhythm and listening so Spanish stops sounding "too fast" and starts sounding familiar.

You will also discover that real conversation runs on a small set of reusable structures. When those structures are stable, vocabulary sticks more easily, grammar becomes supportive instead of paralyzing, and mistakes stop derailing you. You will learn how to control conversations, repair errors without killing flow, and ask questions that shift pressure away from you. You will train your ear for accents, slang, and real-world noise so understanding doesn't collapse outside ideal conditions.

None of this happens through long, heroic study sessions. It happens through deliberate, repeatable action. Twenty to forty minutes a day is enough when those minutes are designed correctly. Weekly checkpoints will show you what is changing and what needs adjustment. Missed days will not break the system, because the system is built for real life, not ideal schedules.

By the time you reach real-life scenarios—travel, work, social life—you will no longer be improvising from scratch. You will be recognizing patterns you have already practiced. Situational fluency will replace abstract confidence. You will know how to order, negotiate, connect, and recover when things go wrong. You will stay in Spanish longer because you trust yourself more, not because you force yourself to.

This is not a promise of effortless fluency. Effort is required. Discomfort will appear. But the discomfort will be purposeful, contained, and temporary. You will no longer wonder whether you are "doing it right." You will see the feedback. You will feel the difference week by week.

The real advantage of sixty days is not the number. It is the identity shift it creates. When you speak every day, even briefly, Spanish stops being something you aspire to and becomes something you do. Fear loses authority. Hesitation shortens. Flow begins to appear in moments you didn't plan.

You are not here to finish a book. You are here to become someone who speaks. The pages that follow are not a curriculum to survive, but a system to inhabit. If you commit to the structure, show up imperfectly, and stay engaged, Spanish will stop being a problem to solve and start being a skill you live.

That is the 60-day advantage.